H.G. Wells

WHO WROTE THAT?

LOUISA MAY ALCOTT, SECOND EDITION
JANE AUSTEN
AVI
L. FRANK BAUM
JUDY BLUME, SECOND EDITION
RAY BRADBURY
BETSY BYARS
MEG CABOT
BEVERLY CLEARY
ROBERT CORMIER
BRUCE COVILLE
SHARON CREECH
ROALD DAHL
CHARLES DICKENS
DR. SEUSS, SECOND EDITION
ERNEST J. GAINES
S.E. HINTON
WILL HOBBS
ANTHONY HOROWITZ
STEPHEN KING
URSULA K. LE GUIN
MADELEINE L'ENGLE
GAIL CARSON LEVINE
C.S. LEWIS, SECOND EDITION
LOIS LOWRY
ANN M. MARTIN
STEPHENIE MEYER
L.M. MONTGOMERY
PAT MORA
WALTER DEAN MYERS
ANDRE NORTON
SCOTT O'DELL
CHRISTOPHER PAOLINI
BARBARA PARK
KATHERINE PATERSON
GARY PAULSEN
RICHARD PECK
TAMORA PIERCE
DAVID "DAV" PILKEY
EDGAR ALLAN POE
BEATRIX POTTER
PHILIP PULLMAN
MYTHMAKER: THE STORY OF J.K. ROWLING, SECOND EDITION
MAURICE SENDAK
SHEL SILVERSTEIN
LEMONY SNICKET
GARY SOTO
JERRY SPINELLI
R.L. STINE
EDWARD L. STRATEMEYER
MARK TWAIN
H.G. WELLS
E.B. WHITE
LAURA INGALLS WILDER
JACQUELINE WILSON
LAURENCE YEP
JANE YOLEN

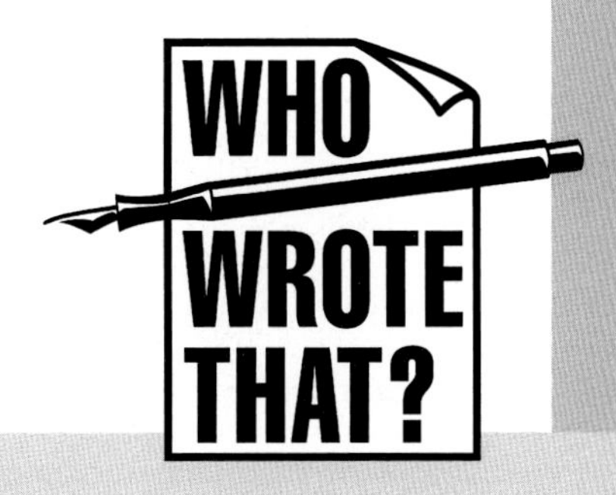

H.G. Wells

Dennis Abrams

Foreword by
Kyle Zimmer

H.G. Wells

Chelsea House
An imprint of Infobase Learning
132 West 31st Street
New York, NY 10001

Library of Congress Cataloging-in-Publication Data
Abrams, Dennis, 1960–
H.G. Wells / by Dennis Abrams.
p. cm. — (Who wrote that?)
Includes bibliographical references and index.
ISBN 978-1-60413-770-5 (hardcover)
1. Wells, H. G. (Herbert George), 1866–1946—Juvenile literature. 2. Novelists, English—20th century—Biography—Juvenile literature. 3. Science fiction—Authorship—Juvenile literature. 4. Children's stories—Authorship—Juvenile literature. I. Title. II. Series.
PR5776.A65 2011
823'.912—dc22
[B] 2010030588

Chelsea House books are available at special discounts when purchased in bulk quantities for business, associations, institutions, or sales promotions. Please call our Special Sales Department in New York at (212) 967-8800 or (800) 322-8755.

You can find Chelsea House on the World Wide Web at http://www.infobaselearning.com.

Text design by Keith Trego
Cover design by Alicia Post
Composition by EJB Publishing Services
Cover printed by Yurchak Printing, Landisville, Penn.
Book printed and bound by Yurchak Printing, Landisville, Penn.
Date printed: April 2011
Printed in the United States of America

10 9 8 7 6 5 4 3 2 1

This book is printed on acid-free paper.

Table of Contents

FOREWORD BY
KYLE ZIMMER
PRESIDENT, FIRST BOOK

HUMANITY IS POWERED by stories. From our earliest days as thinking beings, we employed every available tool to tell each other stories. We danced, drew pictures on the walls of our caves, spoke, and sang. All of this extraordinary effort was designed to entertain, recount the news of the day, explain natural occurrences—and then gradually to build religious and cultural traditions and establish the common bonds and continuity that eventually formed civilizations. Stories are the most powerful force in the universe; they are the primary element that has distinguished our evolutionary path.

Our love of the story has not diminished with time. Enormous segments of societies are devoted to the art of storytelling. Book sales in the United States alone topped $24 billion in 2006; movie studios spend fortunes to create and promote stories; and the news industry is more pervasive in its presence than ever before.

There is no mystery to our fascination. Great stories are magic. They can introduce us to new cultures, or remind us of the nobility and failures of our own, inspire us to greatness or scare us to death; but above all, stories provide human insight on a level that is unavailable through any other source. In fact, stories connect each of us to the rest of humanity not just in our own time, but also throughout history.

This special magic of books is the greatest treasure that we can hand down from generation to generation. In fact, that spark in a child that comes from books became the motivation for the creation of my organization, First Book, a national literacy program with a simple mission: to provide new books to the most disadvantaged children. At present, First Book has been at work in hundreds of communities for over a decade. Every year children in need receive millions of books through our organization and millions more are provided through dedicated literacy institutions across the United States and around the world. In addition, groups of people dedicate themselves tirelessly to working with children to share reading and stories in every imaginable setting from schools to the streets. Of course, this Herculean effort serves many important goals. Literacy translates to productivity and employability in life and many other valid and even essential elements. But at the heart of this movement are people who love stories, love to read, and want desperately to ensure that no one misses the wonderful possibilities that reading provides.

When thinking about the importance of books, there is an overwhelming urge to cite the literary devotion of great minds. Some have written of the magnitude of the importance of literature. Amy Lowell, an American poet, captured the concept when she said, "Books are more than books. They are the life, the very heart and core of ages past, the reason why men lived and worked and died, the essence and quintessence of their lives." Others have spoken of their personal obsession with books, as in Thomas Jefferson's simple statement: "I live for books." But more compelling, perhaps, is the almost instinctive excitement in children for books and stories.

Throughout my years at First Book, I have heard truly extraordinary stories about the power of books in the lives of children. In one case, a homeless child, who had been bounced from one location to another, later resurfaced—and the only possession that he had fought to keep was the book he was given as part of a First Book distribution months earlier. More recently, I met a child who, upon receiving the book he wanted, flashed a big smile and said, "This is my big chance!" These snapshots reveal the true power of books and stories to give hope and change lives.

As these children grow up and continue to develop their love of reading, they will owe a profound debt to those volunteers who reached out to them—a debt that they may repay by reaching out to spark the next generation of readers. But there is a greater debt owed by all of us—a debt to the storytellers, the authors, who have bound us together, inspired our leaders, fueled our civilizations, and helped us put our children to sleep with their heads full of images and ideas.

WHO WROTE THAT? is a series of books dedicated to introducing us to a few of these incredible individuals. While we have almost always honored stories, we have not uniformly honored storytellers. In fact, some of the most important authors have toiled in complete obscurity throughout their lives or have been openly persecuted for the uncomfortable truths that they have laid before us. When confronted with the magnitude of their written work or perhaps the daily grind of our own, we can forget that writers are people. They struggle through the same daily indignities and dental appointments, and they experience the intense joy and bottomless despair that many of us do. Yet somehow they rise above it all to deliver a powerful thread that connects us all. It is a rare honor to have the opportunity that these books provide to share the lives of these extraordinary people. Enjoy.

Young English cricketers ready themselves for a game, during H.G. Wells's boyhood in the 1860s. Wells sustained an injury while playing cricket as a child that forever altered his future. During his convalescence, he began to read widely and found that he had a love of literature and writing.

1

Two Turning Points

LIFE IS FILLED WITH turning points—events that happen that can change the course of one's life. Sometimes something minor brings about such a change. A snap decision to join Little League or to take a dance class can lead to a lifelong love of sport or dance, or even to a career. A teacher's interest can encourage and inspire a student to take classes he or she had never imagined taking. A chance meeting can bring about a friendship that lasts a lifetime.

Other turning points can be more dramatic. The great Indian leader Mohandas Karamchand Gandhi had studied and planned to become an attorney. While living in the racially segregated nation of South Africa, however, he was thrown off a train at the town of Pietermaritzburg after refusing to move from the first-class car to third-class coach, despite having a ticket for first class.

As Gandhi was continuing on his journey by stagecoach, a driver beat him for refusing to travel on the footboard to make room in the coach for a European passenger. Then he was barred from staying in certain hotels. Finally, when the magistrate of a Durban court ordered him to remove his turban, something he refused to do, he knew his life had changed. Instead of practicing law on his own, his experience, that turning point in his life, awoke him to the cause of social injustice and pushed him into a life of social and political activism.

At the turn of the twentieth century, very few women went to college, let alone women who were blind and deaf. So, if Helen Keller had not become ill as an infant and lost her sight and hearing, would she have ever felt the need to test herself to the utmost and become the first blind and deaf student ever to graduate from Radcliffe College?

An attorney becomes the hero of Indian independence and the father of nonviolent protests. A small-town Southern girl becomes a Radcliffe graduate and a champion for the rights of the blind and deaf. The path that your life is *supposed* to take can change in an instant, on an accident, in a fateful moment, on almost anything at all. The life of British author Herbert George Wells, best known as H.G. Wells, was no different.

A LIFE-CHANGING INJURY

As a child of the lower-middle class growing up in the small town of Bromley, in the county of Kent, England,

H.G. Wells had his future pretty well laid out for him. He would get some education—not too much—but enough so that he could read and write at a basic level. From there, his choice of careers would be severely limited. He would start by serving as an apprentice to a tailor perhaps, or maybe a chemist (also known as a pharmacist) if he seemed to have an inclination for science.

After completing his apprenticeship, he would go on to serve as a clerk in a shop of some kind, marry and have children, and probably live and die in the same town he had grown up in, the same town where his own children would follow in the same path. In nineteenth-century England—today known as Victorian England after the era's long-reigning monarch, Queen Victoria—there was a place for everybody and everybody had his or her place. To go beyond one's expected place took a tremendous amount of intelligence, drive, and luck.

According to Wells, his life was filled with turning points, what he called in his autobiography "starts in life"[1]—events that helped propel him in an altogether different direction than his station in life might have dictated. The first major turning point occurred when he was just seven years old. He described the event in his memoirs, *Experiment in Autobiography*, knowing full well that the incident had forever changed him: "My leg was broken for me when I was between seven and eight. Probably, I am alive to-day and writing this autobiography instead of being a worn-out, dismissed and already dead shop assistant, because my leg was broken."[2]

While playing cricket, the son of his family's landlords, the Suttons, trying to be friendly, picked up young Herbert George and playfully tossed him in the air, asking him,

"Whose little kid are you?"[3] Unfortunately, Herbert wiggled out of place, the landlord's son was not able to catch him, and Herbert wound up with a shattered shinbone.

Herbert was carried home from the field. In those days, all doctors could do was set and strap the broken leg between splints and wait for it to heal. It was a long period of convalescence for the boy, but fortunately for Herbert, and for generations of readers to come, fate came through the door bearing gifts that would inspire the future author his entire life. He recalled:

> [F]or some weeks I found myself enthroned on the sofa in the parlour as the most important thing in the house, consuming unheard-of jellies, fruits, brawn and chicken sent with endless apologies on behalf of her son by Mrs. Sutton, and I could demand and have a fair chance of getting anything that came into my head, books, papers, pencils, and toys—and particularly books. I had just taken to reading.

Did you know...

The game of cricket is, after soccer (otherwise known as football in the rest of the world), the world's second most popular sport. A game played by two teams of 11 players each using a bat and a ball, cricket probably originated in southern England in the sixteenth century. Within 200 years, it had become Britain's most popular sport. As the British Empire expanded throughout the world, cricket followed, and today, the International Cricket Council has 105 member countries.

> I had just discovered the art of leaving my body to sit impassive in a crumpled up attitude in a chair or sofa, while I wandered over the hills and far away in novel company and new scenes. And now my father went round nearly every day to the Literary Institute in Market Square and got one or two books for me, and Mrs. Sutton sent me some books, and there was always a fresh book to read. My world began to expand very rapidly, and when presently I could put my foot to the ground, the reading habit had got me securely. Both my parents were doubtful of the healthiness of reading, and did their best to discourage this poring over books as soon as my leg was better.[4]

A simple beginning: A young boy with a broken leg and time to kill turns to books to fill the long hours. But what he discovered in books, and the way that reading expanded his world, was the start, the spark that lit a fire within him. And despite his parents' attempts to discourage him, he kept on reading.

Why would anybody's parents *discourage* him or her from reading? The answer is both simple and deeply sad. His parents believed with absolute certainty that their son would grow up to be nothing more than a clerk in a store. Given that fact, reading, and dreaming of a better life was, in their eyes, simply a waste of time.

Fortunately for the history of literature, Wells did not stop reading and did not stop dreaming of a better life. Just 22 years after he had broken his leg, with the publication of his first novel, *The Time Machine*, in 1895, H.G. Wells was a best-selling author, one whose series of groundbreaking science fiction novels, including *The Island of Dr. Moreau*, *The Invisible Man*, *The War of the Worlds*, *When the Sleeper Wakes*, and *The First Men in the Moon*, have expanded the worlds of generations of readers.

If Wells's sole contribution to literature and the world had been his science fiction titles, that alone would have been enough to ensure him literary immortality. But for the "father of science fiction," there was much more. He wrote a series of "serious" comic novels, including *Kipps*, *Tono-Bungay*, and *The History of Mr. Polly*, which closely examined Britain's lower-middle classes and their struggle for better lives. He wrote histories of the world and histories of science. He wrote books predicting what the future would hold. He wrote books that explained the changes that he felt that individuals as well as governments needed to make to build a fair and just society.

In these books, the author's dream of a better life for himself expanded ever outward to include a dream of a better life for everyone, of a society that did not serve to crush the dreams of those less fortunate. He knew he had been lucky to break out of the role that society had determined for him. To achieve a fair and just society, others would have to break out as well, even if that meant changing society to do it. He wrote:

> But when a man has once broken through the paper walls of everyday circumstance . . . he has made a discovery. If the world does not please you *you can change it*. . . . You may change it to something sinister and angry, to something appalling, but it may be you will change it to something brighter, something more agreeable, and at the worst something much more interesting. There is only one sort of man who is absolutely to blame for his own misery, and that is the man who finds life dull and dreary.[5]

How did the son of a failed shopkeeper and a domestic servant burst free from his perceived destiny to become one of the most famous writers of his time? How did the young man who failed at every apprenticeship his parents tried to place him in go on to become the author of more than 50 novels, 90 short stories, 70 works of nonfiction, three screenplays, and countless articles, essays, and lectures?

To learn the answer to that, we must go back to the beginning, to a "handsome great house"[6] called Up Park, where a young ladies' maid named Sarah Neal met and fell in love with a young domestic gardener named Joseph Wells.

Sarah Wells, the mother of H.G. Wells, was a domestic servant. Her hard life and devout beliefs would help to shape her son's thinking on society at large.

2

Early Childhood

My mother was a little blue-eyed, pink-cheeked woman with a large serious innocent face. She was born on October 10th, 1822, in the days when King George IV was King, and three years before the opening of the first steam railway. It was still an age of horse and foot transit, sailing ships and undiscovered lands.[1]

—H.G. Wells

HER NAME WAS Sarah Neal, the daughter of a Midhurst innkeeper and his often-ill wife. Because her mother was frequently confined to her bed, it often fell to Sarah to help run the inn: setting the tables, and drawing and serving large tankards of beer from the bar.

In those days, going to school was not mandatory. In 1833, however, when Sarah was 11 years old, her father came into some money and sent his daughter to a finishing school for young ladies in nearby Chichester. There, she learned the subjects that it was felt necessary for a well-brought-up young girl to know, as her son explained years later in his autobiography:

> [S]he learnt to write in the clear angular handwriting reserved for women in those days, to read, to do sums up to, but not quite including, long division, the names of the countries and capitals of Europe and the counties and county towns of England (with particular attention to the rivers they were "on") and from Mrs. Markham's History all that it was seemly to know about the Kings and Queens of England. Moreover she learnt from Magnell's Questions the names of the four elements (which in due course she taught me), the seven wonders of the world (or was it nine?), the three diseases of wheat, and many such facts which Miss Riley deemed helpful to her in her passage through life.[2]

Much to Sarah's disappointment, though, she did not get the opportunity to study French because it cost extra, and her father did not want to pay for it. On the other hand, the religious training she received at Miss Riley's served to reinforce the Protestant piety she had absorbed from her sickly mother. Her son later pointed out:

> She was given various edifying books to read, but she was warned against worldly novels, the errors and wiles of Rome, French cooking and the insidious treachery of men, she was also prepared for confirmation and confirmed, she took the sacrament of Holy Communion, and so fortified and finished she returned to her home.[3]

According to Wells, she believed that "God our Father and Saviour, personally and through occasional angels, would *mind* her."[4] She faithfully believed that God listened to her prayers and that she always had to be good and "not give Satan a chance with her. Then everything would be all right. That was what her 'simple faith' as she called it really amounted to, and in that faith she went out very trustfully into the world."[5] Unfortunately, her faith would not be enough to protect her from all that the world would have to offer.

The formal schooling of Sarah Neal lasted for just three years. Her choice of career was no real choice at all—she would become a lady's maid. Before that could happen, though, there was more for her to learn. She served a four-year apprenticeship as a dressmaker while also learning the art of hairdressing, all designed "to equip herself more thoroughly for that state of life into which it had pleased God to call her."[6]

It was a world very different from what we know today. It was, as her son later described it, a world of "other ladies' maids and valets, . . . upper servants above the level of maids and footmen, a downstairs world, but living in plentiful good air, well fed and fairly well housed in the attics, basements and interstices of great mansions. It was an old-fashioned world."[7]

According to Sarah's diary, which begins in 1845, she worked for the wife of one Captain Forde, with whom she traveled and lived in Ireland and throughout England. In 1850, she became the maid to Miss Bullock of Up Park near Petersfield. Here, she would meet a young gardener who would take her away from her career, and in due time, become the father of one Herbert George Wells.

"HE SEEMS *PECULIAR*"

The future author's father, Joseph Wells, was the son of the head gardener to Lord de Lisle at Penshurst Place in Kent. The Wells family had been in Kent for generations. They were mainly "of the upper-servants, tenant farmer class,"[8] with the exception of one of Joseph's first cousins, who was able to elevate himself in the world through the manufacture of cricket balls and bats.

Joseph Wells grew up gardening and playing cricket, and, in the words of his son, "remained an out-of-doors, open-air man to the day of his death."[9] As a young boy he worked as a gardener for a man also named Joseph Wells (no relation) who treated him kindly, encouraged him to learn to read, and supplied him with books on botany and gardening.

Upon the death of his employer, Joseph Wells went in search of work. In his writing, his son thought that there might have been a lingering sense of disappointment in his father, who he believed was saddened that the old Mr. Wells did not help him to get a start in life. After working for several other employers, Joseph Wells, now 24 years old, was hired as the new gardener at Up Park.

Based on the entries in Sarah's diary, their first meetings were not particularly auspicious. One early entry about him reads, "He seems *peculiar*."[10] But from that weak start, a relationship soon developed, as the gardener and the ladies' maid met at the weekly dances held by candlelight and danced to the music of concertinas and fiddle in the servants' hall. The two undoubtedly saw each other at other times as well, when the gardener would come to the house to discuss the flowers and vegetables needed for the day, or on Sundays on the way to church.

Soon enough, he was showing up in her diary entries as "Joe," and he had given her the pet name of "Saddie." In the spring of 1853, Sarah left Up Park to return home to tend to her mother, who was seriously ill. Joseph not only came to visit her that summer, but he also left Up Park himself and began to look for another place of employment. After Sarah's father died unexpectedly in August of that year and her mother died just three months later, on November 5, Sarah's destiny seemed clear. On November 22, 1853, Sarah Neal married Joseph Wells in London at St. Stephen's Church.

MARRIED LIFE

Shortly after their wedding, Joseph Wells got a job and cottage at Shuckburgh Park in the Midlands. Life there was good, but unfortunately, as Wells commented in his autobiography, "It was to be the happiest and most successful home she ever had, poor little woman."[11] In 1855, for reasons unknown, Joseph Wells was asked to leave Shuckburgh Park and their cottage.

Unable to find work as a gardener, Joseph Wells began to consider starting a small business and becoming his own boss. A cousin, George Wells, owned a small, unsuccessful shop that sold china and crockery in the High Street of Bromley, Kent, and offered to sell it to Joseph for what seemed to be a very reasonable price. Joseph took the gamble, and using all of his savings and reserves, bought what was known as Atlas House. (The shop was named after a statue of Atlas that carried the weight of a lamp on his shoulders instead of the world. The statue was located in the shop window.)

So with his wife and infant son (Wells's oldest brother, Frank), the family moved into 47 High Street, occupying rooms above, below, and behind the ramshackle little shop. The investment proved to be a disaster. H.G. Wells later wrote that "they were caught. From the outset this business did not 'pay,' and it 'paid' less and less. But they had now no means of getting out of it and going anywhere else."[12] It was into this house, this failing shop, and this dead-end situation that Herbert George Wells was born on September 21, 1866.

Did you know...

Although Herbert George Wells grew up during the reign of Queen Victoria and lived through the reign of King George VI, his coming of age as a writer was during the reign of King Edward VII, known as the Edwardian Era.

If the Victorian Era was the period of English expansion and wealth—a period when the gap between the educated upper classes and the uneducated lower classes was at its peak—the Edwardian Era was when that all began to change. Education became more commonly available, workers and women became more politicized, and the rigid lines that made moving from one class to another began to ease. Writers of the Edwardian period, such as Wells, reflected and commented on the changing times, as did other noteworthy authors of the day, including John Galsworthy, Arnold Bennett, E.M. Forster, and P.G. Wodehouse.

GROWING UP POOR

He was the youngest of three sons: Frank was nine years older, and Freddy, four years older. A sister, Fanny, died of appendicitis in 1864, two years before the birth of Herbert, a tragedy from which Sarah Wells never quite recovered. Indeed, Sarah's life was now one of constant struggle, unhappiness, and doubt, as she worked to keep the family's struggling business afloat, raise her children, and maintain a household under the most difficult of circumstances.

In his autobiography, Wells drew careful attention to the house in which he grew up. In the vividness of his prose, he is able to not only make his readers see the house but also to feel what it was like living in such cramped quarters:

> The house in which [I] ran about, clattering up and down the uncarpeted stairs . . . was one of a row of badly built houses upon a narrow section of the High Street. In front upon the ground floor was the shop, filled with crockery, china and glassware and, a special line of goods, cricket bats, balls, stumps, nets and other cricket material. Behind the shop was an extremely small room, the "parlour," with a fireplace, a borrowed light and glass-door upon the shop and a larger window upon the yard behind. A murderously narrow staircase with a twist in it led downstairs to a completely subterranean kitchen, lit by a window which derived its light from a grating on the street level, and a bricked scullery, which, since the house was poised on a bank, opened into the yard at the ground level below. In the scullery was a small fireplace, a copper boiler for washing, a provision cupboard, a bread pan, a beer cask, a pump delivering water from a well into a stone sink, and space for coal, our only space for coal, beneath the wooden stairs. . . .

H.G. Wells at the age of nine. His childhood love of reading sparked his desire to get an education and to become a writer.

We were much too poor to have a servant, and it was more than my mother could do to keep fires going upstairs (let alone the price of coal). Above the ground floor and reached by an

> equally tortuous staircase—I have seen my father reduced to a blind ecstasy of rage in an attempt to get a small sofa up it—were a back bedroom occupied by my mother and a front room occupied by my father . . . and above this again was a room, the boys' bedroom . . . and a back attic filled with dusty crockery stock. . . . [T]here was not a scrap of faded carpet or worn oil-cloth in the house that had not lived a full life of usefulness before it came into our household. Everything was frayed, discoloured and patched. . . .
>
> We lived, as I have said, mostly downstairs and underground, more particularly in the winter. We went upstairs to bed. About upstairs I have to add a further particular. The house was infested with bugs. . . . This was the material setting in which my life began. [13]

Realizing that his family had no way to survive on the earnings from the shop, and with no way of selling the shop, Joseph Wells augmented his family's income as a professional cricket player and instructor. Left alone to run the shop and raise a family, Sarah Wells gradually changed from a prim and proper lady's maid to "a tired woman more and more perplexed by life."[14] The values she had learned at Riley's, and the life she had lived at Up Park, had done nothing to prepare her for the life she was now living.

Her workday never stopped. In the mornings, Joseph Wells would get up and light the fire (a task she was never able to do), and she would then make breakfast while he opened up the shop. Getting the boys out of bed would be her next task, giving them breakfast and sending them off to school. Next was making the bed, washing the breakfast dishes, dusting, and scrubbing the floors. As her son later described it: "There was no O-Cedar mop, no polished floor; down you went to it on all fours with your pail beside you."[15]

If Joseph was out on deliveries or away playing cricket, she would tend to the shop's customers, another task with which she was never comfortable. Then, lunch would have to be made for her and the boys, who came home from school to eat. On many occasions, there was little food. Sometimes the family lived on nothing more than cabbages, potatoes, and beer.

The lunch dishes would then have to be washed, clothes would have to be mended, tea would have to be made, and dinner prepared and cleaned up after. It was only at night, when Joseph Wells had gone out with friends to a local bar and the boys were asleep in their beds that Sarah would have a moment of rest, allowing her to write letters and add to her diary. Wells wrote, "My mother in those days was just the unpaid servant of everybody."[16]

Her life was aging her quickly. She had wrinkles around her eyes, and her mouth had begun to draw in upon itself due to some lost teeth, teeth she was reluctant to replace because to her it "would have seemed a wicked extravagance."[17] Her youngest son often wondered what she was thinking as she sat alone night after night in front of the dying fire, doing her last bits of sewing before going up the "unfortunate" staircase to her bed.

Despite her growing unhappiness and religious doubts caused by the death of her daughter and the never-ending drudgery of her life, she was determined to raise Herbert George with the same religious values she had been brought up with. Those, she believed, combined with daily doses of cod liver oil and an unwillingness to let him play with what she saw as "common children,"[18] would ensure that her youngest son would live a good and pious life.

Young Herbert, though, would have none of it. A rebel from an early age, he had begun to see the world in a very different way from his parents. And when his broken leg brought him full-force into the world of books, his life would never be the same again.

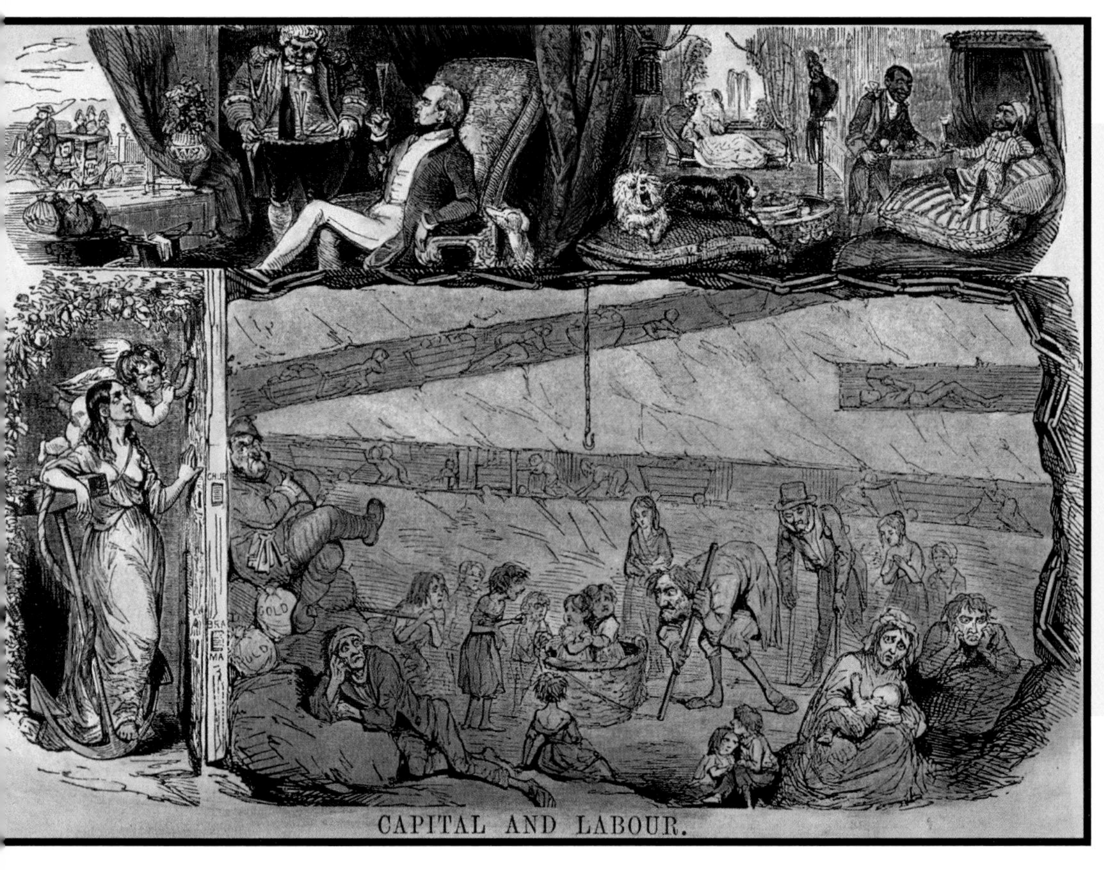

This 1843 cartoon from Punch, *a British magazine, was inspired by a British government report on the horrific state of workers in coal mines. The stark division between the rich and poor in Great Britain would influence much of H.G. Wells's writing, including his depiction of the Eloi and the Morlocks in* The Time Machine.

3

Early Education

YOUNG HERBERT GEORGE WELLS had learned to read from his mother, who taught him the alphabet using a big sheet of capital letters decorating the underground kitchen. She taught him his numbers from the same sheet. She taught him to count up to 100. She taught him the rudiments of writing: *Butter* was the first word he ever wrote.

When she had taught him all she could, she sent him off with his older brother Freddy to a nearby school, run by "an unqualified old lady, Mrs. Knott, and her equally unqualified daughter Miss Salmon."[1] There he learned weights and measures, learned to read words longer than two syllables, and tried but failed to learn addition and subtraction.

But, laid up in bed with a broken leg, without the modern world's distraction of radio, television, and computers, he was able to fully enter the realm of books, of ideas, of the world. He never looked back.

He wrote years later: "I cannot recall now many of the titles of the books I read, I devoured them so fast, and the title and the author's name in those days seemed a mere inscription on the door to delay me in getting down to business."[2] There was a two-volume book about the countries of the world, a book that took him from Tibet to China, from the Rocky Mountains to Brazil. There was Wood's *Natural History*, from which he developed a "profound fear of the gorilla."[3]

He read about the Duke of Wellington, who defeated Napoleon at the Battle of Waterloo. He read about the American Civil War and studied its battles. He read the works of American author Washington Irving. He read bound volumes of the British magazine *Punch*. He read everything he could get his hands on, everything his father and neighbors brought home for him to read. And through his reading he gained a glimpse of the world outside of Atlas House, of the world outside of Bromley. It was a world that he wanted to know more about.

FIRST SCHOOL

Education would be the road that Wells wanted to follow. At the age of seven (and three-quarters, as he points out in his autobiography), Herbert entered Morley's Commercial Academy, "a rather white-faced little boy in a Holland pinafore and carrying a small green baize satchel for my books."[4]

The school was opened by Thomas Morley in 1849 and was considered slightly old-fashioned, even by the time that Wells enrolled. Morley was "a bald portly spectacled man with a strawberry nose and ginger-grey whiskers, who considered it due to himself and us to wear a top hat, an ample frock-coat, and a white tie, and to carry himself with invariable dignity and make a frequent use of 'Sir.'"[5] He may have appeared dignified, but by today's standards, he was unqualified to own and operate a school.

He was the sole teacher, relying only on the assistance of his wife. The school was one single room, with desks around the walls. The students ranged in age from six to thirteen, each studying different subjects at different times, so maintaining discipline was essential. Morley did not hesitate to hit his students with his hands, with books, with rulers, or with whatever else was handy in order to keep his young charges in line.

The goal of the school was not so much to prepare students for higher education but to prepare them for a lifetime career as a clerk of some kind, perhaps with a specialized interest in bookkeeping. When Herbert left the school at age 13, he had learned the rudiments of mathematics and geometry, along with the beginnings of trigonometry and calculus, and had learned to speak English with "precision."[6]

That, though, was the extent of his education at Morley's, and the most that anyone of his class and station in life was *expected* to learn. Looking back years later, Wells could not remember Morley ever encouraging him to read a book, with the exception of the worn textbooks shared by all the students. It was not the most thorough of educations.

Yet this basic education, designed to prepare him for his allotted place in the world, was not enough for young Herbert George Wells. By 13, he had read enough on his own and thought enough on his own to know that he wanted something more. He knew his own worth and deeply resented both the assumption of what his place in life should be and his mother's deferential attitude to what she saw as her social superiors. Wells wrote that "my resentful heart claimed at least an initial equality with every human being; but it was equality of position and opportunity I was after."[7]

AN EARLY REJECTION OF RELIGION

Along with his rejection of his mother's view of her and her sons' place in the world, he had begun to reject her religious view of the world as well.

Given his mother's strong religious beliefs, Herbert was taught to hold the same convictions as a young boy. He was taught to fear hell and not to question the existence of God. Soon, however, doubts began to emerge. Some of these arose from his own questioning intellect, and some from his observation of his mother, who he felt, even at that age, was experiencing doubts of her own. Sarah's doubts were brought on by the knowledge that her belief and prayers had not saved her daughter's life nor eased or comforted her own unhappy life at Atlas House.

The final straw for Herbert, though, was a dream of hell, one so strange that it made believing in hell impossible for him. Wells had read in an old magazine about the punishment of a man being "broken" on the wheel. One night, he dreamed of God in a "particularly malignant phase, busy basting a poor broken sinner rotating over a fire built under the wheel."[8] In Wells's dream, there was no Satan; God himself was responsible for the poor man's punishment. It was a traumatic experience for Wells, who later wrote: "That dream pursued me into the day time. . . . And then suddenly the light broke through to me and I knew this God was a lie."[9]

For young Herbert, it was the beginning of a withdrawal from all organized religion and the start of his own search for a way to make sense of the world. That search, though, was going to be cut short, as life intruded on the Wells family and dimmed the possibility that he would be able to escape the hand that fate seemed to have dealt him.

ANOTHER BROKEN LEG

One October day in 1877, while the rest of the family was at church (Herbert still attended with his mother, despite his growing doubts), Joseph Wells was pruning a grapevine in the family's backyard. When his wife and children arrived back home, they found him lying on the ground, writhing in pain. He had fallen and shattered his thighbone.

With that, it quickly became clear that Joseph Wells would be "heavily lame for the rest of his life."[10] This was a grievous blow to the family's shaky financial footing. The loss of all the supplemental income earned from Joseph Wells's playing cricket, combined with the additional medical expenses arising from his injury, made life at Atlas House even more difficult than it already was.

Supper was now often nothing more than bread and cheese. The bill for Herbert's education at Morley's Commercial Academy went unpaid. Things at Atlas House began to appear desperate. Suddenly, though, almost miraculously, Sarah Wells received an unexpected offer in 1880. A new housekeeper was needed at Up Park. The new lady of the manor, Lady Fetherstonhaugh, for whom Sarah had been a maid when she was Miss Bullock, had long thought well of her onetime servant and offered her the job.

It would mean breaking up the family. Herbert's oldest brother, Frank, had completed his apprenticeship as a

A photo of a slum in London, circa 1890. The failure of his father's business meant that H.G. Wells would be forced to give up his education and become an apprentice in order to help keep the family from abject poverty.

draper and was toiling in a position of his own. Freddy's apprenticeship as a draper was ending, so he would also be in his own position soon. Joseph Wells would stay and tend to Atlas House. But what of Herbert?

With the family's finances in ruins, his parents believed the time had come for him to end his education and follow in his brother's footsteps. As Wells later said about his mother, "Almost as unquestioning as her belief in Our Father and Our Saviour, was her belief in drapers."[11] Sarah Wells was determined that her son, too, would be a draper, that "to wear a black coat and tie behind a counter was the best of all possible lots attainable by man—at any rate by man at our social level."[12] An apprenticeship was quickly found with Messrs. Rodgers and Denyer. It was a crushing blow for Wells. He later wrote in his autobiography: "Now it was my turn to put the things away, put the books away, give up drawing and painting and every sort of free delight, stop writing stories and imitations of *Punch*, give up all vain hopes and dreams, and serve an employer."[13]

HIS FIRST APPRENTICESHIP

During his apprenticeship, Herbert stayed in the men's dormitory—a room with 10 beds and four washstands, along with one "dismal little sitting room"[14] with one window that opened up on a blank wall, where he and his fellow apprentices were allowed to sit during their evenings.

Days were spent in the shop. Every morning he would come down from the dormitory at 7:30, dust the shop, clean the windows, eat a simple breakfast of bread and butter, and prepare his work for the day. He was assigned the task of sitting on a tall stool where he would take money in, give change, enter the amounts on a sheet, and stamp receipts. After the shop closed, he would sweep out the shop and have just a couple of hours to himself before the lights went out in the dormitory at 10:30.

This would be his schedule, his life, day after day, six days a week, every week of the year: One day a week the shop closed early at five, and Sundays were his own. It was not the life he had dreamed of having, definitely not the life he wanted for himself. It was the life that was *expected* of him, the life his brothers had already fallen into. He was miserable.

He did not, as he put it his autobiography, rise to the demands put upon him. Although his body was there on the stool, his mind was always somewhere else, dreaming about something better. He would smuggle books to read while sitting at his desk or do algebra problems to help keep his mind occupied. But he was careless about giving out change, and the figures he entered into his cash sheet were often wrong, out of "sheer slovenliness."[15]

After less then a year into his apprenticeship, his mistakes began to catch up with him. Based on the constant errors in his bookkeeping, he came close to being accused

Did you know...

H.G. Wells suffered through several failed apprenticeships. Do you know what being an apprentice meant?

In Wells's time, before vocational or technical schools, people learned a trade directly from a practitioner. Upon signing papers with the tradesman (and often providing him with a payment as well), the apprentice would receive "on the job" training from his employer, who taught his trade and provided room and board. In exchange, the apprentice provided cheap labor for the employer by working for him during the training and for a set period of time afterward.

of stealing from the company, before those in charge realized that he was simply bad at his job and not cut out to be a draper.

For the time being, he had won a respite from his mother's dream of his becoming a draper, of becoming something respectable. His father tried to get him a position with one of his old cricketing acquaintances, but to no avail. Fortunately for Herbert, however, fate once again stepped in. Alfred Williams—a distant relative nonetheless known as "Uncle" Williams—had been a teacher in the West Indies and was about to become the head of a village school at Wookey. He was willing to bring Wells to the school as an "improver," a pupil-teacher who would teach the younger students while taking classes himself. The goal was that, upon graduation, he would go on to a training college.

It was a way out. Wells could escape the life of an apprentice and resume his education. Needless to say, he jumped at the opportunity. Unfortunately for Herbert, though, this means of escape would last just three months.

A portrait of H.G. Wells at age 13, shortly before he arrived at his mother's home at Up Park, where he was again exposed to a rarified world of books and learning.

4

Student/ Apprentice/Teacher

UNCLE WILLIAMS WAS, by any definition, an interesting character. H.G. Wells describes him in his autobiography as

> an active centrally bald yellow-faced man with iron grey whiskers, a sharp nose, a chin like the toe of a hygienic slipper, and glasses. Extraordinary quantities of hair grew out of his ears. He had lost one arm, and instead he had a stump in which a hook was screwed, for which a dinner fork could be substituted.[1]

He was also a political freethinker and rogue, a man who helped Herbert develop a new way of looking at the world. "He gave me a new angle from which to regard the universe,"

Wells said later. "I had not hitherto considered that it might be an essentially absurd affair, good only to laugh at."[2] Unfortunately, Williams was also a bit of a liar and had exaggerated his qualifications to run a national school to the government. By May 1881, he was fired from the school; Herbert had already been sent to live with his mother at Up Park until something else could be found for him.

LIFE AT UP PARK

Herbert was only 14 years old when he arrived at Up Park, a failed draper's apprentice and the victim of his uncle's lies. Entering his mother's domain at Up Park opened his eyes to a new world, one of wealth and privilege. It was one where, in his eyes, education and rational thought were the highest qualities that mankind could achieve.

Indeed, it became one of his most firmly held convictions that modern civilization had been born and nurtured in households such as this one, where, free from the pressure of having to work for a living, "men could talk, think and write at their leisure. . . . They, at least, could go on thinking and doing as they pleased."[3] It was this life at Up Park, the world that Sir Matthew Fetherstonhaugh represented, that became the basis for the future author's own Utopian dreams for society and for the cultured, educated elites who would rule.

For Herbert, Up Park gave him entry into a world of books and art and science that he had only previously dreamed of. Sir Fetherstonhaugh saw something in the young man and encouraged him to take advantage of Up Park's assets. There were beautiful art books filled with engravings of the Vatican paintings of Raphael and Michelangelo for him to pore over. There was a telescope that he was allowed to bring into his bedroom to point out his window and look at the skies on those clear, cold winter nights.

There was also the estate's private library to explore, where he could find the books he had always wanted to read but had never had access to. He learned to speak French by reading Voltaire. He read *Vathek* by William Beckford and *Rasselas* by Samuel Johnson, dove into the books of the American Revolutionary War thinker Thomas Paine, and "devoured"[4] Jonathan Swift's satirical masterpiece, *Gulliver's Travels*.

Did you know...

The Republic, **written by the Greek philosopher Plato, did not influence only H.G. Wells. It remains—more than 2,000 years after it was written around 380 B.C.—one of the most influential books of all time.**

Written as a dialogue (almost in the form of a play), ***The Republic*** **is a discussion between the philosopher Socrates (who had been Plato's teacher) and a group of Athenians and foreigners. Among the topics under discussion are: What is justice? Is a just man happier than the man who is unjust?**

Other topics include a proposal that society be ruled by an elite group of philosopher-kings, whether the soul is immortal, and what roles the poet and the philosopher should serve in society. Plato's best-known work, it is a book that can be read over and over again, for its insights into human nature, as well as to help understand its influence on philosophy and political theory throughout the Western world.

And most important, he read Plato's *The Republic*. In the Greek philosopher's work, Plato imagines a just society and how government should work. Without knowing it, Herbert had found the book he was seeking. *The Republic* proved to him that society was not permanent; that the world he found so oppressive could, indeed, be changed. It was another turning point in his young life. Wells later recalled:

> I found Plato's *Republic*. That . . . was a very releasing book indeed for my mind. I had learnt the trick of mocking at law and custom from Uncle Williams . . . but here was something to carry me beyond mockery. Here was the amazing and heartening suggestion that the whole fabric of law, custom and worship, which seemed so invincibly established, might be cast into the melting pot and made anew.[5]

FALSE STARTS

Unfortunately, Herbert could not live at Up Park forever. He would have to move on and forge a path in life. His mother set him up as an apprentice to Mr. Samuel Cowap, a chemist in Church Hill, Midhurst, just a few miles from Up Park. He enjoyed the work and was a good employee, but lasted for a only few weeks. When he found out the cost to qualify as an assistant and dispenser of drugs, he realized that it was beyond his mother's ability to pay. Something else would have to be found.

Two good things did come out of the experience, though. Many years later, he drew upon his time at the shop and the personalities of its owners, Mr. and Mrs. Cowap, when writing his novel *Tono-Bungay*. In addition, because any qualified druggist needed to speak at least some Latin, Mr. Cowap had arranged for his apprentice to take lessons in Latin from Horace Byatt, the headmaster of the Midhurst Grammar School.

Up Park, the home of Sarah Wells while she worked as a domestic servant, was built between 1685 and 1695. Here, H.G. Wells came to believe that education was one of the most important things for a young man to gain.

When Herbert's apprenticeship came to its rapid end, Byatt took him in as a boarder, encouraging his obviously gifted student to shift from Latin to science, a subject in which he would be able to earn his keep by receiving grants for his studies. It was an ideal opportunity for Herbert, allowing him to escape from his "solitary dreamland"[6] and to enter the world of other students, of education, and of ideas being discussed and debated.

Sarah Wells, however, unable to see her son's true worth, was unwilling to give up on her dream of a career in drapery for him. After just six weeks at Midhurst, Herbert learned that his mother had arranged for him to leave the school and apprentice with Edwin Hyde, the proprietor of the Southsea Drapery Emporium on Kings Road in Southsea.

He was heartbroken at the news and tried everything he could to change his mother's mind. But faced with her tearful pleadings, and without the ability to stay in school on his own, he gave in. In May 1881, he set off for Southsea to begin his one-month trial. The following month, his articles of apprenticeship were signed, and Herbert George Wells, who had gotten a glimpse of a better life at Up Park and at Midhurst, was entering what he called "the most unhappy hopeless period"[7] of his life.

SOUTHSEA DRAPERY EMPORIUM

He was jealous of those boys who, despite being no better than him, had the advantages of going to public school and university, getting the chance they deserved. At Hyde's, he was working 13 hours a day. While the apprentices were provided with a good housekeeper, decent food, and access to a small collection of books, Herbert, not surprisingly, despised his time there. For two years, he just went through the motions, certain that his last chance at happiness was gone. He was, he thought, finally and forever trapped in a life in the retail trade.

"The unendurable thing about it," he wrote in his autobiography, "was that I was never master of my own attention. I had to be thinking continually about pins and paper and packages."[8] For the young dreamer and thinker, who wanted nothing more than time to read, it was an unbearable situation.

That he was not cut out to be a draper was evident to everyone around him. He was, in the words of his biographers Norman and Jeanne MacKenzie, close to having a nervous breakdown. In his mind, his life had come down to three choices: accepting his lot in life and being miserable, suicide (which he never really seriously considered), or "an escape from the suffocating situation which he found intolerable."[9] But with his father still tied down by a bad leg and a failing business at Atlas House, and his mother and older brothers eager for him to start his career as a draper, it would be up to him to find his own way out of the trap that life had laid out for him.

He wrote to his mother, to his father, to his brothers, begging for help. He wrote to Mr. Byatt at Midhurst begging for help. Byatt wrote back with an offer: If Herbert was able to pass an exam, he could work at Midhurst as an assistant teacher, while taking classes on his own. It was, in Herbert's view, an offer he could not refuse.

Sarah Wells, though, was harder to convince. Not only was she worried about her son's future, there was the matter of the £40 that had been paid for the cost of Herbert's apprenticeship. If he broke the terms of the agreement, that money would be lost. Letters were written among all the members of the family, meetings were held, tears were shed. Finally, Herbert went to Up Park to plead his case.

Once again, he had returned as a failed apprentice. He pleaded his case to his mother, and, backed up by a better offer from Byatt of a guaranteed income of £20 for the first year, with an increase to £40 thereafter, Sarah Wells gave in. Herbert would leave Southsea to return to Midhurst. And his mother would give up on her dreams of a respectable career as a draper for her son.

The two most difficult years of his life were over. It had been, however, extremely useful to him. Wells later wrote that it was "so bad a time as to stiffen my naturally indolent, rather slovenly and far too genial nature into a grim rebellion against the world—a spurt of revolt that enabled me to do wonders of self-education before its force was exhausted."[10]

For the rest of his life, he was grateful to Byatt who, he said, made him "suddenly wake up to the existence of a vast and growing world of thought and knowledge outside my ordinary circle of ideas altogether."[11] For the next year, Herbert devoted himself wholeheartedly to the task of catching up on all the time he had lost.

During the day, he taught the school's younger students under Byatt's watchful supervision. By night, he hit the books, studying every science textbook Byatt could give him. Herbert—whose interest in science had begun when he had read Wood's *Natural History* at the age of seven while recovering from his broken leg—found that not only was it a subject he was interested in, but one that proved remarkably easy for him to learn.

It was a win-win situation for student and teacher. For Herbert, it was the chance to get the education he had always wanted. For Byatt, his apprentice's accomplishments would help to pay the bills: The school received a £4 grant for every advanced pass in a given subject.

When examinations were given in May, Herbert won several awards for the school, enough to earn back more than Byatt had paid out in room, board, and salary for his young student. In fact, from Byatt's perspective, Herbert may have done too well. As part of a government plan to train science teachers, scholarships were offered for pupils who scored well in their exams to attend the Normal School of Science in South Kensington. Herbert George Wells was one of the scholarship recipients. Byatt had taken his young prodigy as far as he could. It was time for him to leave Midhurst and test himself at one of the nation's finest schools.

The British biologist Thomas Henry Huxley was a prominent supporter of Charles Darwin's theories on evolution. He also greatly influenced the thinking of one of his students, H.G. Wells.

5

His Education Continues

The day when I walked from my lodging in Westbourne Park across Kensington Gardens to the Normal School of Science, signed on at the entrance to that burly red-brick and terra-cotta building and went up by the lift to the biological laboratory was one of the great days of my life.[1]

—H.G. Wells

HERBERT GEORGE WELLS WAS 18 years old when he arrived in London in September 1884 to attend the Normal School of Science. The school had only been open for five years. Even so, the Normal School, known today as the Royal College of Science, had already established itself as the center for the study of evolutionary biology—the new branch of science that took a giant leap forward with the publication of Charles Darwin's *On the Origin of Species* in 1859. Through this book, one of the most important in the history of scientific literature, Darwin proposed theories that changed the way we looked at the world.

What exactly did Darwin propose? He said that the world we live in, the plants, the animals, the human beings, all the living things around us, are not the same as they were when life on Earth first began. All of these organisms changed, or *evolved*, over time, through a process known as natural selection. Darwin wrote that life forms adapt to their environment: Those less suited to the environment are less likely to survive and less likely to reproduce. Those suited to their environments are more likely to survive, to reproduce, and to pass on the traits that they inherited and that helped them survive to their offspring. Natural selection, the process by which the strong survive and the weak do not, is also known as survival of the fittest.

Darwin's theory, which states that all living things on Earth, including people, change and evolve and improve over long periods of time, stood in opposition to some of the most widely held beliefs of the day. To most people in the Western world, life on Earth did not change, did not evolve, and existed as it always had since life began, just as it said in the Book of Genesis in the Bible. Such a difference of opinion produced a vigorous debate between those who interpreted the creation story in the Book of Genesis literally and supporters of Darwin's work.

One such debate took place at Oxford University on June 30, 1860, a mere seven months after the publication of *On the Origin of Species*. Many of Britain's best-known scientists and philosophers participated, including Thomas

Henry Huxley and Bishop Samuel Wilberforce. Today, the debate is best known for a heated exchange between Huxley and Wilberforce, one that greatly served to increase Huxley's fame among Britain's intellectual elite.

By 1879, just a few years before Wells arrived at the Normal School, Huxley—known as "Darwin's bulldog" for his ardent support of Darwin's theories—had brought together a number of the science departments originally part of the Royal School of Mines and established the Normal School as a center for science teaching. It would be here that the new science of evolution would be taught, research would continue, and the science teachers of the future would be trained.

For Wells, it was as though he had come "from beginnings of an elementary sort to the fountainhead of knowledge."[2] Before this, all of his education, everything he had learned about science, had come from books. Now, for the first time, he had access to the real thing: microscopes, dissections, models, diagrams, museums, and most importantly, professors who most likely had many of the answers to his questions.

Wells took two classes with Professor Huxley: elementary biology and zoology. He spoke to him only once, holding open the door for him and saying, "Good morning."[3] Yet, Wells later wrote, "That year I spent in Huxley's class was, beyond all question, the most educational year of my life."[4] It was not only Huxley's skill as a teacher that enthralled Wells; he fell under his spell completely. His biographers Norman and Jeanne MacKenzie wrote that Wells "remained so, emotionally and intellectually, to the end of his days."[5]

What he learned from Huxley was simple: "Man must struggle for survival and that a mere slip of fortune might doom all his hopes."[6] It was a lesson that Wells knew all too well from his own life. He knew how hard he had had to struggle and to fight for his own start in life. And he knew all too well how a single slip of fortune, such as his father's broken leg, could doom the hopes of an entire family.

This idea of the struggle for survival, of a fight for physical and social progress, was one that affected Wells deeply for the rest of his life. It was a curious mix of ideas: his belief that man was evolving and that society could progress and change with the assistance of science, blended with his feeling that mankind was also being held back in its progress by its animal origins and the violence that was still all too much a part of human nature.

In February 1889, Professor Huxley wrote an article for the publication *Nineteenth Century* on a term he invented: agnosticism—the belief that an absolute understanding or certainty is unattainable, especially without knowledge based on experience or proof. Moreover, an agnostic doubts the existence of God for the simple reason that it is impossible to have faith in a supreme being without physical evidence or actually seeing God with one's own eyes.

At the conclusion of his article, Huxley struck a point that can be seen as a summation of much of Wells's own thoughts. Here the future author's agnosticism, or doubt, can be seen to apply not only to a belief in a deity, but also to the idea of the hope for man's progress. Huxley wrote:

> I know of no study which is so utterly saddening as that of the evolution of humanity. Man emerges with the marks of his lowly origin strong upon him. He is a brute, only more intelligent than the other brutes, a blind prey to impulses . . . a victim to endless illusions, which make his mental existence a burden, and fill his life with barren toil.[7]

Throughout Wells's life, he struggled with these two ideas: that progress is made possible by science and that progress is at the same time made impossible by humanity's imperfections.

STRUGGLES

Although Wells flourished in his first year under Huxley's tutelage, he struggled in the next. Taking physics with Professor Guthrie, Wells, whose interest ran in different directions, began to question whether he would be able to stick it out long enough to become a teacher. His work suffered: One piece of equipment that he built was so badly made that it was kept on display in the lab for years as an example of what *not* to do.

At the end of the term, the question of whether his scholarship would be extended was in serious doubt. And if that was not enough stress for the young Wells, two years of living in near poverty (the small stipend he was receiving was hardly adequate) were making their mark on his physical appearance and health. His weight fell to just 112 pounds (51 kilograms), and in his own words, he was "in a shocking state of bodily unfitness, very thin, under-exercised and with no muscular dexterity, loose in gesture, slow on the turn and feeble in the pouch."[8]

Of course, given the schedule and diet he described in his autobiography, his physical appearance was no surprise: "I was as light and thin as I have said, because I was undernourished. I ate a hastily poached egg and toast in the morning before going off for my three mile [4.8-kilometers] tramp to the schools and I had a meat tea about five when I got back—and a bread and cheese supper."[9]

There was, however, one bright spot in his life at this point: Wells discovered the school's debating society. The meetings were held in a theater used by the mining school, lit by only one or two gas jets. For almost half an hour, one person would present a paper on his position on a given topic, followed by loud and "promiscuous"[10] discussion. Those who were too afraid to speak were still able to make their voices heard by pounding on their desks "until the ink jumped out of the pots."[11] For a young man with as many strong and rapidly evolving opinions as Wells, it was the perfect place to work those ideas out.

There was, however, one problem: Religion and politics were considered off the table and not fit subjects for debate, and "the rest of the universe"[12] was left to the mercy of the debaters. For Wells, this was totally unacceptable, as he explained in his autobiography:

> I objected to this taboo of religion and politics. I maintained that these were primary matters, best beaten out in the primary stage of life. I did all I could to weaken and infringe those taboos, sailing as close to the wind as possible. . . . One evening someone read an essay on *Superstitions* and cited among others the thirteen superstitions. I took up the origin of that. "A certain itinerant preacher whom I am not permitted to name in this gathering," I began, "had twelve disciples . . ."[13]

Needless to say, a "debate" sprang up that lasted for nearly an hour and ended only when Wells was physically carried, still struggling, from the proceedings. But this was the sort of scene that Wells was beginning to enjoy. He liked to make provocative statements and be irreverent. He loved "making strange unsuitable noises, the wailing of a rubber blowpipe tube with its lips stretched, for example, and in provoking bursts of untimely applause."[14] In his own words, "it seems to me that I must have been a thoroughly

A circa-1896 colorized photograph of H.G. Wells as a young author. His writing was greatly shaped by his experiences as a student at the Normal School of Science.

detestable hobbledehoy at this stage, a gaunt shabby candidate for expulsion."[15]

Indeed, his interest was rapidly moving from science into politics and literature. For Wells, learning about "the past, present and implicit future of the planet"[16] began to take a backseat to his efforts to understand the idea of socialism—a political and economic theory that advocated common ownership and cooperative management of the means of a society's industrial and agricultural production. And his interest in working in a laboratory was rapidly being replaced by an interest in the thoughts and writings of others. He remarked:

> I was doing my best to find out what such exalted names as Goethe and Carlyle, Shelley and Tennyson, Shakespeare, Dryden, Milton, Pope—or again Buddha, Mahomet and Confucius—had had to say about the world and what they mattered to me. I was learning the use of English prose and sharpening my mind against anyone's with whom I could start a discussion.[17]

At this stage in his life, the majority of those discussions were about politics and his developing belief in socialism. While his beliefs grew and changed over time, their essence remained the same. Because of his impoverished childhood, because of the role he had been expected to play in society, Wells understood all too well the basic unfairness of a society in which there were haves and have-nots, with no expectation that things would ever or *could* ever change.

So Wells embraced the possibility of completely changing the system as it was through political philosophies like socialism. If life itself could change and evolve, why not society in general? He wrote in his autobiography: "Men asked fiercely why should things always be thus and thus when as a matter of fact they had only just become thus and thus and were bound to alter in any case. 'Let us have a new world,' they said and they called it Socialism."[18]

Did you know...

THE FABIAN SOCIETY AND E. NESBIT

Because of his socialist beliefs, H.G. Wells was, for a period of time, a member of the Fabian Society, one of Great Britain's most prominent socialist movements. Among its members were many of Britain's leading intellectual and artistic figures, including George Bernard Shaw, Leonard and Virginia Woolf, Sidney and Beatrice Webb, and the writer Edith Nesbit. Although Wells's membership in the Fabian Society was cut short by arguments over policy, he established long-lasting personal relations with many of its members, including Nesbit.

But who is Edith Nesbit? Known as E. Nesbit, she is one of the greatest, and yet most overlooked, authors who wrote for children and young adults. Called the first modern writer for children, Nesbit took child characters and placed them in situations that combined both the reality of their times with magical objects and travels to beautifully imagined fictional worlds. A major influence to writers such as P.L. Travers, C.S. Lewis, and J.K. Rowling, she is an author who deserves to be rediscovered. One of her most well-known books is *The Story of the Treasureseekers.*

He came to believe in a classless society, in which people were judged and allowed to progress not on their wealth or place in society but on their individual merits. The way to achieve that, he felt, was through a world-state, with one government running the world, a government that would rule human activities with an eye toward the common good. He dreamed of a world without individuals competing to earn the most money and possessions, of a world without nations competing against nations for land. He imagined a world perfected, a world that had evolved though planning and science.

Whether such a world is possible or even desirable is a completely different question. What is important is the way that Wells's beliefs, in evolution, in science, and in socialism, affected his life and his work. In fact, his work, even his science fiction novels and social novels, served as a way for him to share with the world his beliefs about society's faults and the ways it could be changed for the better.

Those pioneering works of science fiction, though, were still years in the offing. He was still a student, still studying science, and still uncertain of his future. Even so, in the summer of 1886, in a letter he wrote to a friend, he included a cartoon drawing of himself, surrounded by scraps of papers covered with proposed subjects like "How I Could Save the Nation," "All About God," and "Wells' Design for a New Framework for Society."

Indeed, writing was beginning to become his primary focus. He wrote a paper for the debating society, "The Past and Present of the Human Race," a piece that anticipates descriptions of characters in such later works as *The First Men in the Moon* and *The War of the Worlds*. Along with a group of friends, he founded and edited the *Science Schools*

Journal, for which he wrote, among other pieces, "The Chronic Argonauts," a story that eventually was reborn as *The Time Machine*.

The 1886–1887 school year was his last at the Normal School of Science. Despite passing his exams in biology and physics, his complete lack of interest in geology led, unsurprisingly, to his failure to pass the class, and he lost his scholarship. Once again, Wells found himself without a job, without a source of income, and at a loss for where to go next. Fortunately, a family member was ready to lend a hand.

He went to live with his Aunt Mary, who, with her sister, ran a small boardinghouse. Aunt Mary had a daughter, Isabel, who worked at a photography shop retouching pictures. Wells quickly became infatuated with his cousin, but as a young man with little to offer, it seemed unlikely to him that anyone would fall in love with him, let alone agree to marry him.

So when a teaching position opened up at the Holt Academy in North Wales, Wells packed his bag and left London. The position had seemed promising, but when he arrived, he found a school on its last legs, with "a group of dingy buildings, catering to a handful of children of farmers and shopkeepers, and some candidates for the ministry who were 'three lumpish young men apparently just off the fields.'"[20]

For one month, he coped with the disappointing conditions as best he could by improving class lessons, teaching religion (despite his feelings on the subject) on Sundays, taking advantage of finally having enough to eat, and trying to improve his physical condition by playing cricket and soccer with the students. It was not a difficult schedule, and he used his free time to the utmost, writing voluminous letters and trying his hand at writing short stories. It seemed likely to Wells that he could easily settle down into "the role of a second-rate secondary teacher. I should have awakened one day to find myself thirty and still in a school dormitory."[21]

ANOTHER INJURY

While playing soccer on August 30, 1887, Wells had yet another mishap that changed his life. An opposing player put his shoulder under Wells's knees and sent him flying. Wells got up and tried to continue to play but was too hurt to go on. With a tremendous pain in his side, he returned to the house, his ears ringing with the mocking yells of the students. What happened next was both horrifying and unbelievable. He recalled in his autobiography:

> In the house I was violently sick. I went to lie down. Then I was moved to urinate and found myself staring at a chamber-pot half full of scarlet blood. That was the most dismaying moment in my life. I did not know what to do. I lay down again and waited for someone to come. . . . The next day a doctor was brought from Wrexham. He discovered that my left kidney had been crushed.[22]

Wells stayed in bed as long as he could recovering, but to receive his salary he had to go back to work, at least through December. He went back to teaching, but within weeks, a bad cough he had been nursing for some time grew worse. Wells discovered that his lungs seemed to be following his kidney's lead "and that the handkerchief into which I coughed was streaked with blood."[23] The small-town doctor at Wrexham declared in no uncertain terms that Wells was a consumptive suffering from tuberculosis, which, in those days, was generally fatal. Despite this death

Isabel Mary Wells was the cousin and first wife of H.G. Wells. They were married in 1891 and had no children.

sentence, Wells remained at Holt through Christmas, determined that, at the very least, he would earn the £20 he had been promised.

Then, no longer able to teach and without income or hope, Wells returned once again to his mother's care at Up Park. He remained there for four months, slowly convalescing from his kidney and lung problems. At first he was close to despair at his fate, a fear of remaining an invalid, a fear of never being able to accomplish anything, a fear of being trapped:

> There was also a considerable amount of pure fear in my mind, a sort of claustrophobia, for though I disbelieved intellectually in immortality, I found it impossible to imagine myself nonexistent.
>
> I felt I was going to be stifled, frozen and shut up, but still I felt I should know of it. I had a nightmare sense of the approach of this conscious nothingness.[24]

His health had its ups and downs before a new doctor happened to be a guest at Up Park and took Wells under his care. Dr. Collins determined that Wells was not suffering from tuberculosis and that he could be cured. With the knowledge that he would not be trapped by his condition or by a shortened life, Wells returned to the world of mental activity, spending his hours reading, writing, and thinking abundantly.

For the first time in years, he began carefully reading poetry and novels, which he had generally shunned earlier. Knowing that he was no longer physically capable of a long-term career in teaching, Wells was more and more certain that writing was going to be his means of escaping the life he was supposed to live. To do it well, however, he knew he would have to learn how others before him had done it:

> I was reading and reading poetry and imaginative work with an attention to language and style that I had never given these

> aspects of literature before. I was becoming conscious of the glib vacuity of the trash I had been writing hitherto. When I look back on my life, there is nothing in it that seems quite so preposterous as the fact that I set about writing fiction for sale, after years of deliberate abstinence from novels or poetry. Now, belatedly, I began to observe and imitate.[25]

Like almost any writer before and after him, Wells was learning a valuable lesson. It is not enough to want to know how to write. To be a writer, you have to read everything, good and bad, to see how things are done and how they should not be done. Lessons learned, Wells read over "with shame"[26] everything that he had previously written and burned almost all of it. He knew that before he had been playing at writing, scribbling for the amusement of himself and his friends. Now, he knew, it was time to take writing seriously.

The time had come, though, when he once again had to leave Up Park. He left to stay with his school friend and the onetime co-editor of the *Science Schools Journal*, William Burton, and his new wife, waiting for opportunity to show up at the Burtons' door. Unfortunately for Wells and the newlywed Burtons, opportunity rarely goes out and finds one—it has to be sought out. Wells remained with the Burtons probably longer than he should have. Finally realizing he had overstayed his welcome, and using the last £5 in his possession, Wells set out for London, looking to make a new start.

A circa-1890s portrait of Herbert George Wells at the beginning of his literary career. The novels he would write as a young man have endured for more than a century.

6

The Writer Awakens

NOW 22 YEARS OLD and still without any serious prospects, H.G. Wells moved to London hoping to finally make a success of his life. He wrote, "I have given up counting my starts in life. This return to London was, I suppose, about the seventh or eighth in order."[1] For four shillings a week, he rented a portioned-off part of an attic, with no fireplace, a simple bed, a washstand, a chair, and a small chest of drawers with a mirror. From this spartan base of operations, Wells set out to conquer London.

It was a slow and painful process. Work was impossible to find. Soon, Wells was in desperate straits, his £5 nearly gone.

One evening he examined his pockets and found nothing there but a pencil eraser, a pocketknife, and a halfpenny. And, as he pointed out, even in those days when money went much further, there was "nothing in the way of supper to be done on a halfpenny."[2] Indeed, he had already had to stop sending postcards: At three farthings each, keeping up with his correspondence was just too expensive.

Fortunately, Wells ran into an old schoolmate, A.V. Jennings, who was lecturing on biology at the Birkbeck Institute. Jennings needed a collection of wall diagrams for his work, and remembering that Wells had a certain talent in that direction, hired him to make copies of diagrams from textbooks. Wells leaped at the chance, and with the knowledge that he had a certain amount of money coming in, he left the half attic he had been living in and rented a room from his Aunt Mary. There, he could live a more comfortable existence, and, as an added benefit, was reunited with his cousin Isabel, for whom he still held very strong feelings.

Wells continued to work for his friend Jennings while doing some tutoring on the side. He continued to court Isabel, with whom he had settled into a relationship akin to an engagement. And to top things off, he received an offer to teach at the Henley House School, a private school owned by J.V. Milne. Wells would be in charge of the science department and was given free rein to run it as he saw fit.

Although he knew that teaching was not going to be his long-term career, Wells took the position, but with a few stipulations. Since he wanted to remain living with his aunt and cousin, he refused to live at the school, offering to arrive at nine and "vanish at or before five."[3] He would not teach any religious classes, feeling that, since he was no longer a believer, he could no longer do so in good conscience.

Wells's stipulations were accepted, and he taught at Henley House for more than a year. One of his students was the owner's son, A.A. Milne, who years later became famous for his literary creation, Winnie the Pooh. Although Wells enjoyed his time at Henley House and did a good job, the position meant that he was giving up on his dream of writing. "During 1889, my 'efforts' to write," Wells said in his autobiography, "so far as I can remember or trace them now, died down to hardly anything at all. My hope of an income from that source had faded, and it seemed to me that such prospects in life as remained open to me, lay in school teaching."[4]

With that in mind, Wells took his Intermediate Science Examination in July 1889, receiving second-class honors in zoology. At the end of the year, he earned his diploma of licentiate from the College of Preceptors. This in turn earned him a raise from J.V. Milne, as well as a reduction of his hours at Henley House. He supplemented his income as a teacher by working as a tutor for the University Correspondence College at Cambridge.

Wells found the work at the Correspondence College agreeable, and, after finally receiving his degree with first-class honors in zoology and second-class honors in geology, he left Henley House and accepted a permanent position at the Correspondence College, working 50 hours a week tutoring other students to pass their university exams.

Wells settled into the life of teaching he had long resisted, while only partially satisfying his need to be a writer by editing the school's house journal, the *University Correspondent*; editing the College of Preceptors' paper, the *Educational Times*; and writing for other educational papers. For a time, it seemed that, although he had not made his name as a writer, things were finally going Wells's way.

Once again, however, his body revolted. He suffered another lung hemorrhage, which, followed by a serious bout with influenza, forced him to hire someone else to take over his classes, leading to a serious loss of income. But he soon recovered and was able to return to work full time.

Once again armed with a steady income, Wells was able to fulfill his fiancée's desire for a house of her own. On October 31, 1891, he married Isabel Mary Wells in Wandsworth Parish Church. At long last, his personal life and his professional life seemed to be falling into place. But within just years, both his marriage and his career as a teacher would come to an end, to be replaced by a new love and the start of his new life as a writer.

A NEW LOVE, A NEW LIFE

Wells's biographers Norman and Jeanne MacKenzie pinpointed the aspect of his character that led to the changes. Wells loved Isabel, "but once that bond had been formally tied he felt an inarticulate desire to cut it and set himself free."[5] Although she had been the focus of all of his romantic aspirations for years, after marrying her "she became the gently firm champion of all that I felt was suppressing me."[6]

It became a pattern. Whenever Wells began to make a place for himself, he began to feel trapped and feel that he would need to flee in order to survive. Events were about to occur, however, that would strengthen his need to flee to new levels.

In November 1892, Sarah Wells was let go from her position at Up Park and was forced to live with her estranged husband for the first time in years. Wells's brother Fred

A portrait of Amy Catherine Wells, the author's second wife, circa 1897. Married in 1895 after Wells divorced his first wife, they had two sons together: George Philip (known as Gip) in 1901 and Frank Richard in 1903.

was also dismissed from his job as a draper, and, unable to find another position, immigrated to South Africa, where he remained for most of his life. H.G. Wells was now the true head of his family.

Meanwhile, in the school term beginning in the autumn of 1892, he met a young woman among his new students, Amy Catherine Robbins, who was a "fragile figure, with very delicate features, very fair hair, and very brown eyes."[7] She was working to get her degree so she could become a high school teacher. The two quickly struck up a relationship, and within a short period of time, Wells found himself in love with Amy, while still married to Isabel.

Partially to distract himself from the difficult personal situation he found himself in, and partially to ward off his increasing boredom as a correspondence tutor, he again turned to writing. A year earlier, in 1891, Frank Harris's *Fortnightly Review* had published his paper, "The Rediscovery of the Unique." Soon after, Wells sent Harris another article, "The Universe Rigid." An attempt to describe time as the fourth dimension (the other three dimensions being length, width, and depth), the article drew a stunned response from Harris, who summoned Wells to his office to tell him in no uncertain terms that he had no intention of publishing the piece.

Wells was so upset at Harris's rejection that he gave up on writing such ambitious pieces for an entire year. Instead, he confined himself to writing minor articles for educational papers that would accept his pieces without a struggle. Unfortunately, those papers paid so badly it was hardly worth the effort. (Ironically, after Harris heard praise from Irish playwright Oscar Wilde about "The Rediscovery of the Unique," Wells was one of the first authors Harris brought on as a regular contributor when he became editor of the *Saturday Review* in 1894.)

Frustrated with his life and marriage, Wells turned to Robbins for support, intellectual conversation, and, increasingly, for love. He wrote in his autobiography, "It came to me quite suddenly one night that I wanted the sort of life that Amy Catherine Robbins symbolized for me and that my present life was unendurable."[8]

He knew that writing was his way out of his current situation, but he was having a difficult time deciding on a topic that would interest him and find a receptive audience. He found the way to go one afternoon when, recovering from yet another lung hemorrhage, he came upon what he called the "hidden secret"[9] in a book by J.M. Barrie (best known today as the author of *Peter Pan*) called *When a Man's Single.* In the book, one of the characters explains the way to write journalism that will sell:

> "You beginners," said the sage Rorrison, "seem able to write nothing but your views on politics, and your reflections on art, and your theories of life, which you sometimes even think

Did you know...

H.G. Wells enjoyed other forms of artistic impression besides writing. He also was an artist, drawing sketches that served as the endpapers and title pages for his diaries. The subjects of his works ranged from politics and his feelings about other writers to his many romantic interests.

During his marriage to Amy Catherine Robbins, he drew a large number of these pictures, many of them obvious commentary on their marriage and relationship. During this period, he referred to his sketches or cartoons as "picshuas," and they have become a topic of study for Wells's scholars. A book, *The Picshuas of H.G. Wells: A Burlesque Diary*, gives them the careful consideration that they deserve.

> original. Editors won't have that, because their readers don't want it. . . . You see this pipe here? Simms saw me mending it with sealing-wax one day, and two days afterward there was an article about it in the *Scalping Knife*. . . . He has had my Chinese umbrella from several points of view in three different papers. . . . Once I challenged him to write an article on a straw that was sticking to the sill of my window, and it was one of the most interesting things he ever did. Then there was the box of old clothes and other odds and ends that he promised to store for me when I changed my rooms. He sold the lot to a hawker for a pair of flower-pots, and wrote an article on the transaction. Subsequently he had another article on the flower-pots; and when I appeared to claim my belongings he got a third article out of that."[10]

For the struggling young author, it was a revelation, like a lightbulb had suddenly been turned on in his head. He later wrote:

> Why had I never thought in that way before? For years I had been seeking rare and precious topics. "Rediscovery of the Unique!" "Universe Rigid!" The more I was rejected the higher my shots had flown. All the time I had been shooting over the target. All I had to do was lower my aim—and hit.[11]

And hit he did, aided by a bit of fortunate timing. The American millionaire W.W. Astor had just purchased the British *Pall Mall Gazette* and hired an editor, Harry Cust, who was determined to make the *Gazette* "the most brilliant of recorded papers."[12] Everybody in Britain's literary world was enlisted to help, and every contribution offered—from beginners to established authors—was to be taken seriously.

It was the perfect situation for Wells. He had been recovering from his lung relapse in the seaside resort of Eastbourne. Taking Barrie's advice to heart, he quickly wrote an article "On Staying at the Seaside" on the back of a letter and envelope and sent it off to a cousin for her to typewrite. After submitting it to the *Pall Mall Gazette*, it was immediately accepted for publication, as was a second piece, a look at the future entitled "The Man of the Year Million." Article after article followed in a steady and then rapidly increasing stream. His career as a journalist was off to a rousing start.

In retrospect, it seemed to Wells that all of his previous writing, for the *Science Schools Journal*, the *University Correspondent*, the *Educational Times*, the *Journal of Education*, even the countless letters he had written to family and friends, had indeed been just practice. Now, when the time had finally come to make a career as a writer, he was prepared. As he phrased it, "I found myself with the knack of it."[13]

He knew he had been lucky, as he wrote to a friend in 1919:

> Earning a living by writing is a frightful gamble. It depends neither on knowledge nor literary quality but upon secondary considerations of timeliness, mental fashion and so forth almost beyond control. I have been lucky but it took me eight years, while I was teaching & then doing anxious journalism, to get established upon a comfortably paying footing.[14]

Now that he had finally become the writer he had dreamed of being, he was prepared to make other changes in his life as well. Shortly after Christmas of 1893, Wells walked away from his marriage to Isabel and moved in with Amy Catherine Robbins in January 1894. At that time, it was unthinkable for a man and a woman to live together without the benefit of marriage. But Wells and Robbins both valued their freedom and love more than they did society's approval or disapproval.

For perhaps the first time, Wells was satisfied with his life. His work was being regularly published; he had no shortage of ideas of what to write about, indeed the very process of writing excited him. Articles, ranging from "A Stray Thought in an Omnibus" to "My Abominable Cold" to more serious articles such as "The Extinction of Man" and "The Rage of Change in Species" to early stories such as "The Stolen Bacillus," "The Lord of the Dynamos," and "The Flowering of the Strange Orchid" flew off his pen and directly to most of Britain's most important newspapers and journals. In 1894 alone, he sold at least 75 articles, five stories, and one serial. It was a remarkable literary outpouring. But he wanted more.

Wells went to meet with the editor of the *National Observer* to discuss possible writing assignments. He said, "I resolved to do my best for him and dug up my peculiar treasure, my old idea of 'time-travelling.'"[15] For years, he had been tinkering with his original story, "The Chronic Argonauts," and was convinced that he could work on it, expand on it, and make it into something truly special, now that he had come into his own as a writer.

But Wells's initial lucky streak as a writer was about to come to an end. W.E. Henley, the editor of the *National Observer*, was replaced, and the new editor had no interest in "time travel." At the same time, Wells had written so many articles that many of his usual outlets were overstocked with his work and were reluctant to purchase anything new from him. To make matters even worse, Astor announced that he would be closing down the *Pall Mall Gazette*, one of Wells's regular sources of revenue.

Money quickly became a source of difficulty at the Wells household, and their problems continued to grow when their landlady learned that they were living together without being married and tried to do what she could to drive them out of their apartment.

It was W.E. Henley who came to their rescue. He was starting a new journal, *The New Review*, as a monthly, and he wanted to run what Wells was now calling "The Time Traveller" (later to be published as *The Time Machine*) as a serial, running one chapter per issue. He would pay £100 for the right to do so. On top of that, Henley also found a publisher, William Heinemann, who promised to publish the story in book form once its serialization was complete. He would pay an advance of £50 and a royalty of 15 percent—an extraordinarily generous offer for a still largely unknown author.

Wells set to work, knowing that this was his golden opportunity. He wrote, "It's my trump card and if does not come off very much I shall know my place for the rest of my career."[16] Little did he know that the work would become a sensation and would establish him as one of the founding fathers of science fiction.

An illustration from an early edition of H.G. Wells's seminal work of science fiction, The War of The Worlds *(1898), which was one of the first novels to depict a battle between human beings and a race from another world.*

7

The Scientific Romances

OF H.G. WELLS'S SCIENCE fiction, British author Ford Madox Ford wrote, "It did not take us long to recognize that here was Genius. Authentic, real genius. And delightful at that."[1] What had appealed to the public's imagination, was, in Ford's opinion, "Mr. Wells' brand of Science. . . . Fairy tales are a prime necessity of the world, and he and science were going to provide us with a perfectly new brand. And he did. And all Great London lay prostrate at his feet."[2]

It was as though all of his studies, all of his struggles, all of his life had led him to this point. He was ready to write and eager to make his mark on world literature. But there was something else that made the time right for him. Wells was in a unique position, as Richard Hauer Costa explained in his study of Wells:

> The convergence of the biggest idea of the nineteenth century—the theory of evolution—with a mind that was capable of grasping and extending it in all its biological, philosophical, social, and poetical ramifications made possible the earliest— the best-known writings of H.G. Wells.[3]

In 1959, many years after Wells first began his career as a writer, the author C.P. Snow gave what became a famous and influential lecture at Cambridge University, entitled "The Two Cultures." In it, he proclaimed that there was a breakdown of communication between what he called the two cultures of modern society—the sciences and the humanities—which was a roadblock to solving the world's problems. Artists believe they have solutions and ideas on how to fix the world. Scientists are certain they have solutions and ideas on how to fix the world. But if neither group can speak the other's language, how can they communicate?

H.G. Wells was one of the very few writers who was able to bring these two groups together. In rapid succession, from 1895 to 1898, Wells published six novels: *The Time Machine*; *The Wonderful Visit*; *The Wheels of Chance*; *The Island of Dr. Moreau*; *The Invisible Man*; and *The War of the Worlds*, along with most of his short stories. In them, he used his background as a scientist to explore the ramifications of evolution, both past and present, and his growing skill as a writer to turn his ideas into art.

THE TIME MACHINE

The first of these works, 1895's *The Time Machine*, remains one of Wells's most famous and best-loved books.

From today's perspective, with time travel being a common motif in books and movies and on television, it is difficult to understand the truly groundbreaking impact the work had on readers at the end of the nineteenth century. It was, to them, a glimpse at worlds they had never imagined possible.

At the same time, *The Time Machine* is a thrilling and exciting read. It opens at the home of a man who is identified only as "the Time Traveller," whom the reader meets as he is explaining to his guests his theory of time as the fourth dimension. He then shows his friends a machine he has built—the Time Machine.

A week later, the narrator and other guests return to the Traveller's house, where they are amazed to hear about the Traveller's trip forward in time. He had, he claimed, gone to the year 802,701, where he found that the valley of the Thames River had become a garden and the city of London had completely disappeared with the exception of a few crumbling palaces of granite, marble, and aluminum.

Not only had London vanished, but man himself had changed, evolving into two races: the Eloi and the Morlocks. The Eloi were childlike, small, and slender. With the exception of a girl named Weena, whom the Traveller saves from drowning, the Eloi have very little interest in him or his machine. The machine mysteriously disappears, leaving the Traveller with the very real possibility of being trapped forever in the year 802,701.

While desperately searching for his machine, he learns about the existence of the Morlocks, an untamed, nearly wild people who live in caves and passageways carved underneath the Earth's surface. The Morlocks, once dominated by the Eloi, still feed and clothe them. But as the Eloi evolved, they also became the *prey* of the Morlocks, who come out from their underground lairs at night to feast on the flesh of the terrified Eloi.

After many exciting encounters with the Morlocks, during one of which Weena is killed, the Traveller regains possession of his machine (which the Morlocks had hidden away) and makes his escape, traveling once again into the future. Thirty million years have passed, and Earth is now a nearly dead planet, with little surviving except for some sparse vegetation, giant white butterflies, and monstrous crab-like creatures.

He continues to go forward in time, watching as the Earth's rotation gradually stops and the sun grows dimmer, until finally the world falls silent and frozen and the last creatures die out, with the exception of one remaining life form, about the size of a football, trailing its tentacles against the blood-red water.

The Traveller returns home to London in time for the scheduled dinner with his friends who, not surprisingly, have trouble believing his story, calling it "a gaudy lie."[4] A few days later, equipped this time with a knapsack and a camera to capture evidence of his time travels, he once again takes his Time Machine into the future. He is never seen or heard from again.

It was a story that had never been told before. In it, Wells introduced for the first time the idea of time travel and the fourth dimension, ideas that Wells was speculating on years before Albert Einstein published his own theory of relativity. He also presented to the reading public the evolutionary theories of Professor Huxley, all wrapped up in the trappings of an exciting science fiction adventure. (Wells was also, at least as far as can be determined, the man who invented the idea of using a machine to travel through time.)

In *The Time Machine*, the Traveller at first believes that the society of the Eloi, seemingly peaceful and with all their needs met, was an ideal society. For millennia, it seemed, a balance between the "elite" above ground and the workers below ground had been achieved. That balance was destroyed, however, because the Eloi, the "Upper-Worlders," the descendents of the moneyed capitalists of his own day, had ignored Thomas Huxley's most urgent warning: "If we may permit ourselves a larger hope of abatement of the essential evil of the world . . . I deem it an essential condition of the realization of that hope that we cast aside the notion that escape from pain and sorrow is the proper object of life."[5]

Because the ancestors of the Eloi had created a society that gave them security and freedom from danger, they lost their drive, their need to succeed. Their descendants, therefore, over time, evolved into the delicate Eloi. But because the Morlocks are in charge of running the machinery that keeps the society going, they have not evolved in the same way as the Eloi. So when hunger becomes a problem, they are forced to revert to a state of cannibalism to survive.

It was a stunning indictment of a society divided into haves and have-nots. The Time Traveller mused:

> I grieved to think how brief the dream of human intellect had been. It had committed suicide. It had set itself steadfastly toward comfort and ease, a balanced society with security and permanency as its watchword. It had attained its hopes—to come to this at last. Once, life and property must have reached almost absolute safety. The rich had been assured of his wealth and comfort, the toiler assured of his life and work. No doubt in

> that perfect world there had been no unemployed problem, no social question left unsolved. And a great quiet had followed.[6]

The H.G. Wells of this period strongly believed that men had the potential to be both as bestial and cruel as the Morlocks and as unassertive and docile as the Eloi. And it was important for man to remember that, no matter how far he thought he had evolved, both of these extremes were still part of who he was. Linear progress, the idea that evolution would constantly bring forth higher and higher forms of life, was rejected by Wells, who accepted Huxley's belief

Did you know...

H.G. Wells is the lead character in the 1979 movie *Time after Time*.

In the film, Wells himself invents an actual working time machine. When one of his friends is suspected of being Jack the Ripper and uses the machine to escape from the police, Wells follows him to San Francisco, California, in the year 1979.

The movie is a captivating look at a fictional Wells, who is both fascinated with and disappointed by a modern world that did not turn out quite the way he had envisioned. Of course, by the end of the film, Jack the Ripper has been sent tumbling through time with no way to stop, and Wells has fallen in love with a young bank teller who decides at the last minute to return with Wells to his own time. Her name? Amy Robbins, the name of H.G. Wells's real-life second wife!

that evolution was just as likely to bring about, at least for short periods of time, devolution, a regression.

The book was a great success, receiving good reviews and selling more than 6,000 copies in just its first few weeks of publication. Years later, noted British critic V.S. Pritchett stated that *The Time Machine* "will take its place among the great stories of our language."[7] And it is, even with its views of evolution, capitalism, and mankind, one of the most exciting stories ever put on paper.

THE ISLAND OF DR. MOREAU

One of his follow-ups to *The Time Machine* was even more sensational. *The Island of Dr. Moreau*, published in 1896, is, quite simply, one of the more horrific tales ever told. In it, scientist Edward Prendick is shipwrecked and later rescued by an assistant of one Dr. Moreau, who has turned a small island in the Pacific into his own private zoological laboratory. Brought to the island, Prendick finds himself surrounded by strange, grotesque creatures who are semi-human in appearance, yet at the same time obviously jungle animals. They chant a law that Dr. Moreau has taught them:

> Not to go on all-Fours; *that* is the Law
> Are we not Men?
> Not to suck up Drink; *that* is the Law.
> Are we not Men?
> Not to eat Flesh nor Fish; *that* is the Law.
> Are we not Men?
> Not to chase other Men; *that* is the Law.
> Are we not Men?[8]

Initially, Prendick assumes that Moreau's experiments involve turning men into animals, and he fears that he is next. Eventually, though, the truth comes out—Moreau has been experimenting with turning animals into humans by means of surgery. Once again, Wells is showing his readers the pain that mankind goes through as his instincts, his "animal urges," survive even as he slowly evolves into man. "Each time I dip a living creature into the bath of burning pain," Dr. Moreau remarks, "I say, this time I will burn out the animal; this time I will make a rational creature of my own."[9]

By book's end, Moreau is dead, his laboratory has been destroyed, and his creations have taken over the island, already returning to their animal state. Prendick has escaped and returned home to London. There, he looks around him at the "blank expressionless faces of people on trains and omnibuses." What he sees frightens him because "I could not persuade myself that the men and women I met were not also another, still passably human, Beast-People, animals half-wrought into the outward image of human souls."[10] Prendick rightly fears that they, too, might regress, that "they would presently begin to revert, to show first this bestial mark and then that."[11]

It is, obviously, a bleak view of mankind forever on the verge of reverting into our primitive, animal selves. The book appalled critics at the time. The *Speaker* attacked the book for its "originality at the expense of decency . . . and common sense,"[12] while a critic for the *Saturday Review* wrote, "The horrors described by Mr. Wells in his latest book very pertinently raise the question how far it is legitimate to create feelings of disgust in a work of art."[13] Years later, Wells himself described the book as "an excuse in youthful blasphemy. Now and then, though I rarely admit it, the universe projects itself towards me in a hideous grimace . . . and I did my best to express my vision of the aimless torture in creation."[14]

Today, of course, the book is considered one of Wells's finest. For the last 100 years, it has been read, enjoyed, and shuddered over by readers worldwide. It has even been turned into a film three times. Obviously, Wells struck a nerve with his view of the animalistic nature of man, but again, as with *The Time Machine*, his sheer storytelling ability, and the excitement of the story he has to tell, brings readers to his books.

THE INVISIBLE MAN

If *The Island of Dr. Moreau* is one of Wells's most intense and horrified visions of man, then his next book, *The Invisible Man*, is one of his most high-spirited. And even though the book's theme is similar to that of *Dr. Moreau*, its feeling is entirely different.

The Invisible Man is another of Wells's visions of scientific experiments run amok. But instead of an island in the middle of the Pacific, the story takes place in quiet Iping Village in West Sussex. Instead of the evil Dr. Moreau, creating a horrifying world of half men–half beasts, Wells presents us with a man named Griffin, a scientist who develops the theory that *if* a person's "refractive index" can be changed to exactly that of air, and his body is not able to absorb or reflect light, then he will become invisible.

After Griffin carries out the experiment out on himself but is unable to turn visible again, he becomes more mentally unstable as the tale progresses. The humor of the book lies in the balance that Wells achieves between the "unbelievable"—can a man really turn himself invisible?—and the everyday life of the quiet English village in which the story takes place.

To play up this humor, we, the readers, see the Invisible Man through the eyes of the villagers: a man hurrying down

A circa-1902 photo of H.G. Wells seen here in his study at Spade House, Sandgate, Kent, England. At this point in his career, he was beloved for his works of science fiction.

the street covered in bandages and a wig, his mouth nothing but a hole, the pant legs flapping in the breeze, the sleeves empty. The comedy rapidly fades, however, as Griffin becomes more and more convinced that with invisibility comes unlimited power. Once again, Wells seems to be telling us, science, for all the good it does, can easily run amok.

The story ends, as *Dr. Moreau* does, with the death of the scientist. An angry crowd of villagers beats Griffin to death with shovels, and through the eyes of the narrator, Dr. Kemp, we see the Invisible Man becoming merely a man:

> It [the transformation to visibility] was like the slow spreading of a poison. First came the little white nerves, a hazy grey sketch of a limb, then the glassy bones and intricate arteries, then the flesh and skin. . . . Presently . . . his crushed chest . . . the dim outline of his drawn and battered features [and finally] there lay, naked and pitiful on the ground, the bruised and broken body of a young man about thirty . . .[15]

For many, this is one of the most remarkable passages in all of Wells's books. Once again, Wells views humans as being stripped of what makes them human. Once again, Wells is warning us that science is not enough to guarantee human progress. Mankind will always have to be prepared for the worst.

THE WAR OF THE WORLDS

In his next book, *The War of the Worlds* (1898), Wells presented his vision of the worst that could happen. Today, the book is probably best known as the archetype of every science fiction film that presents creatures from outer space invading Earth armed with deadly ray guns. Even so, more than 100 years after its publication, the book still holds a power that remains unsurpassed.

What makes the novel so special is the utter believability with which Wells lays out the story of the Martian invasion of Earth, the conquest of Earth, and life under the Martians.

Wells's childhood interest in war stories combined with his adult vision of how man might react to a Martian invasion made it a story that only he could tell, a story that is all too plausible:

> No one would have believed in the last years of the nineteenth century that this world was being watched keenly and closely by intelligences greater than man's and yet as mortal as his own; that as men busied themselves about their various concerns they were being scrutinized and studied, perhaps as narrowly as a man with a microscope might scrutinize the transient creatures that swarm and multiply in a drop of water.[16]

In Wells's vision, man on Earth was so blinded by his vanity that he could not imagine that intelligent life on Mars not only existed, but had evolved *beyond* that on Earth, and that the Martians, when life on their planet became insupportable, would come in search of another planet to inhabit—Earth.

The Martians are octopus-like creatures (not unlike the aliens Kang and Kodos on *The Simpsons*). They have evolved past human beings in terms of their intelligence and their command of machinery. Once Earth has been invaded, the Martians easily move over the planet in machines of impregnable armor, devastating everything in their path with their Heat-Ray and Black Smoke weapons. The Martians, who live on human blood, give humanity a choice: perish or submit, become as docile as the Eloi, and find refuge underground.

As Richard Hauer Costa points out, "In the robotlike calculations of the Martians, Wells again underscores Huxley: Evolution may produce creatures with superior brains, but it will not inevitably lead to a millennium."[17] Ironically, though, while the Martians' superior brains might not bring about an era of peace, and while man himself may be powerless to stop the conquest, the Martians are finally defeated, by the tiniest of heroes: microscopic bacteria to which they have no immunity.

Once again, as in all of his scientific romances, Wells warns his readers that man has no right to take the control of the cosmic process for granted. He shows his readers how the Martians, faced with dropping temperatures, a thinning atmosphere, and a lack of water, were forced to look elsewhere to save themselves. The same thing, he warned us, nearly a century before climate change threatened Earth, could happen here.

WHAT'S NEXT?

In a sudden burst of literary activity, all the more astonishing given his often poor health, Wells had written an average of one book and 30 stories and articles every six months—more than a million words total. He had examined man's future and displayed his continued mixed feelings about science and his fears of what science could become. Science, he seemed to be saying, is only valuable if it is used to help control the brute that still lurks in man; it is evil if it becomes the servant of man's animal nature.

By 1900, however, Wells's focus began to change. His novels moved from visions of man's past and future, of scientific possibilities and potential disasters, to comic examinations of the life in Britain going on all around him. All the while, Wells's own personal life remained confusing and difficult, a continuing rebellion against the expectations of society.

A circa-1916 photo of H.G. Wells at his desk. In the early years of the twentieth century, Wells began to turn away from science fiction to concentrate on writing nonfiction works about his social beliefs as well as comic novels.

8

The Novelist

AS THE TWENTIETH century began, H.G. Wells, with his health on the upswing, began to feel a new optimism about mankind's future. He seemed no longer convinced, as he appeared to feel in his earlier books, that humanity was doomed. Instead, he now believed that mankind could be saved and that he himself could play a role in its salvation.

In a lecture that he gave at the Royal Institution with the title "The Discovery of the Future," Wells recalled his fear that mankind was destined to perish and that life would end in a dying world:

> That of all such nightmares is the most consistently convincing. And yet one doesn't believe it. At least I do not. And I do not believe in those things because I have come to believe in certain other things, in the coherency and purpose in the world and in the greatness of human destiny. Worlds may freeze and suns may perish, but I believe there stirs something within us now that can never die again.[1]

He entered into this spirit of optimism with his first nonfiction best seller, *Anticipations*, published in 1901. Subtitled "An Experiment in Prophecy," it examined what he imagined the world would be like in the year 2000. It is astonishing to see how many things he got right: He predicted that because of cars and trains, populations would move from the cities to the suburbs; he imagined that both men and women would seek greater freedom in their lives, including greater sexual freedom; and he saw the birth of the European Union.

Did you know...

H.G. Wells loved to play games and was always searching for ways to make them more challenging. War games were among his favorites, so Wells wrote two books, *Floor Games* (1911) and *Little Wars* (1913), to provide them with more structure. Today, *Little Wars* is recognized as the first true recreational war game, and to gamers and hobbyists worldwide, Wells is seen as the father of miniature war gaming.

On the other hand, he also got many things wrong. He did not think that viable aircraft would be available until 1950 and found it difficult to believe that submarines were possible—"my imagination, in spite even of spurring, refuses to see any sort of submarine doing anything but suffocate its crew and founder at sea."[2] Even so, the hits far surpassed the misses, and even more important was his optimism that life, indeed, would be better in 100 years.

Where did his newfound optimism come from? As previously noted, it arose in part because he was going through a period of relative good health. It came, no doubt, from the remarkable success he had achieved with his scientific romances, which had made him one of Britain's best-known writers. And it also came from a settled personal life: In 1895, after receiving a divorce from his cousin Isabel, he married his former student Amy Catherine Robbins (also known as Jane) and had two sons with her, George Philip, born in 1901, and Frank Richard, born in 1903.

With a new confidence in himself and in the future, his writing began to change. Gone for the time being were the scientific romances that had made him famous and rich. In those books, he had examined the nightmares inherent in contemporary science, using time travellers and Martian invasions to make his point. Now, he would look at the nightmares inherent in the human condition.

Wells had not allowed the two nightmares of his own childhood—his father's insolvency and his destiny to work as a draper—to stop him from escaping the role that society had decreed should be his. Through determination and talent, along with a little bit of luck, Wells had forced his way into a world beyond that of a tradesman's shop. With his new works, he would show that such escape was not only possible but necessary, both for the individual and for society as a whole. He wrote of this lesson he learned:

> But when a man has once broken through the paper walls of everyday circumstance . . . he has made a discovery. If the world does not please you *you can change it* altogether. . . . You may change it to something sinister and angry, to something appalling, but it may be you will change it to something brighter, something more agreeable, and at the worst something much more interesting. There is only one sort of man who is absolutely to blame for his own misery, and that is the man who finds life dull and dreary.[3]

His next two novels, *Kipps*, and the book many consider his masterpiece, *The History of Mr. Polly*, would be demonstrations of that idea.

KIPPS

The first of these novels was *Kipps*, published in 1905. In its early chapters, the story of Artie Kipps is startlingly close to that of Wells himself—a young member of the lower-middle class trapped in circumstances outside of his control as the Victorian Era draws to a close:

> When Kipps left New Romney, with a small yellow tin box, a still smaller portmanteau, a new umbrella, and a keepsake half-sixpence, to become a draper, he was a youngster of fourteen, thin, with whimsical drakes' tails at the poll of his head, smallish features, and eyes that were sometimes very light and sometimes very dark, gifts those of his birth; and

> by the nature of his training he was indistinct in his speech, confused in his mind, and retreating in his manners. Inexorable fate had appointed him to serve his country in commerce, and the same national bias towards private enterprise and leaving bad alone, which entrusted his general education to Mr. Woodrow, now indentured him firmly into the hands of Mr. Shalford of the Folkestone Drapery Bazaar.[4]

With the exception of the names, does this passage not strongly remind you of the early life of one Herbert George Wells?

Unlike Wells, though, who escaped the life of a draper by using his brains to earn a series of scholarships, Kipps experiences a different fate. He had grown up an orphan, raised by his aunt and uncle. After finishing his apprenticeship, Kipps is shocked to learn, while reading the newspaper, that he is actually the grandson of a wealthy man. He inherits his grandfather's fortune—£26,000—and is promptly thrown into the world of high society, a world for which Kipps is ill-prepared.

Kipps struggles, has a failed first marriage, a difficult second marriage, and nearly loses his fortune. By the end of the book, though, all is well. Kipps's fortune is restored, his second marriage becomes a happy one, and Kipps and his wife settle down into a quiet village life, with Kipps opening up a small bookstore so that he will have something to do with his life.

Critics were mixed in their response to *Kipps*. Many applauded the book's verve and energy, while noting that Wells's imagination did not seem nearly as engaged with the life of Artie Kipps as it had been in his scientific romances. Others complained as well that, as a writer,

A 1920s photo of H.G. Wells with his second wife, Amy Catherine, and daughter Anna-Jane, whose mother was the British feminist and author Amber Reeves.

Wells seemed to be looking down at his characters with an air of moral and intellectual superiority and did not lend them the necessary sympathy.

The book, though, like everything that Wells wrote at the time, was a huge commercial success. A few years later came the work that many feel is his greatest achievement as a novelist, *The History of Mr. Polly*.

THE HISTORY OF MR. POLLY

Published in 1910, *The History of Mr. Polly* is still as fresh and timeless as ever. It tells the story of one Mr. Polly, the owner of a small shop deeply in debt, married to a distant cousin named Miriam with whom he is no longer in love. Feeling unhappy, bored, and trapped, Polly makes a rather rash decision: He will kill himself and burn down his house, thereby providing his wife with enough money to rebuild and live on through his insurance.

The fire Polly sets is a raging success, burning down not only his shop and house but also several other shops along with it. The suicide is not as successful, being merely a nick on his throat. Polly, seeing what he has done with his fire, risks his own life to save an old woman trapped in one of the other burning shops and becomes the town's hero. Becoming a hero seems to spark something in Polly, so after making sure that Miriam has received the insurance money, he leaves town, eager for new adventures and a fresh start in life.

Instead of remaining trapped in a failing shop, Mr. Polly chooses life. After a series of comic misadventures, he finds work at a riverside inn, and then finds contentment with the innkeeper, a widow whom Wells never names but simply calls the "plump woman." Knowing that Miriam has used the insurance money to open a tearoom, Polly is able to have with the "plump woman" the happy life he had always dreamed of having.

It seems unlikely, of course, that a novel that involves arson, deception (Polly leads Miriam to believe that he had drowned), and wife abandonment could be funny, but somehow Wells pulls it off. The book *is* funny, exuberant, and full of life.

One reason that the book is so successful and shows Wells at the height of his powers as a novelist is, perhaps, that it is a story that is in some ways very personal. Mr. Polly is, in large part, a mixture of both Wells and his father. H.G. Wells, of course, found himself trapped in an unhappy marriage to a cousin, whom he set up in a laundry business after he divorced her. And Joseph Wells, as we know, was also trapped in a marriage that did not always work, and trapped besides, with the ever-failing Atlas House. With Mr. Polly's drive for personal freedom, Wells was expressing the drive that lived in himself as well as his father.

The History of Mr. Polly remains, as American novelist Sinclair Lewis wrote in 1941, as contagious as ever, "the eternal story of the kindly, friendly Little Man, whose heart and courage would anywhere . . . lift him from behind the counter of the Gent's Furnishings Shoppe, and lead him out to find a wayside world that is perpetually new and surprising."[5]

It was, in many ways, the artistic peak of H.G. Wells's career as a writer. Unfortunately for Wells, his career would last for another 36 years, a period in which both his critical and personal reputations would suffer.

In this 1940 photo, H.G. Wells looks out from the balcony of his writing room, across the greenery of Regent's Park. He believed his home was all that a writer's should be, both close to the heart of London and secluded enough for creative thought.

9

The Prophet

TONO-BUNGAY WAS PUBLISHED in 1909, at the peak of Wells's literary and personal reputation. In it, he combines for perhaps the first and last time the three strands of his literary persona: the spokesman for the generation escaping from Victorianism into the modern world; the science-fiction writer who had made the phrase "the shape of things to come" a motto for coming generations; and the comic novelist who wrote about real people, as in *Kipps*.

George Ponderevo, a science student who is called upon by his Uncle Edward to help promote his new invention, narrates the story. The invention is called Tono-Bungay, a harmful stimulant that is sold as a miraculous cure-all. With the success of Tono-Bungay, George's social status quickly climbs, as does George's unease with his new status. His failed marriage is looked at frankly and honestly (unlike most novels of the day), as is his affair with the "modern woman" Effie and his doomed relationship with Beatrice Normandy.

Inevitably, the Tono-Bungay empire goes bust and collapses. George attempts to save his uncle's finances by stealing the radioactive material "quap" from an island near Africa, but fails. After helping his uncle escape from England in an airplane of his own invention, George finds a new career designing battleships for the highest bidder, while Uncle Edward dies alone of fever in France.

Tono-Bungay is an unflinching look at capitalism, at business selling anything it can at any cost, despite the human consequences, as is seen in this early conversation between George and Uncle Edward about Tono-Bungay:

> "Well, George," he said, quite happily unconscious of my silent criticism, "what do you think of it all?"
>
> "Well, I said, "in the first place—it's a damned swindle!"
>
> "Tut! Tut!!" said my uncle. "It's as straight as—It's fair trading!"
>
> "So much the worse for trading," I said.
>
> "It's the sort of thing everybody does. After all, there's no harm in the stuff—and it may do good. It might do a lot of good—giving people confidence. For instance, against an epidemic. See? Why not? I don't see where your swindle comes in."
>
> "H'm," I said. It's a thing you either see or don't see."[1]

But, despite the presence of such well-drawn characters as George and Uncle Edward, the book, unlike *Kipps* and

The History of Mr. Polly, is not a novel of character. The subject of the book was the character of England itself, and Wells shows it in a state of chaos and decline. The optimistic Wells of his comic novels has once again disappeared. In his place, we see Wells the pessimist, seeing the world around him collapsing and with little hope of salvation. "It may be," says George Ponderevo, "I see decay all about me because I am, in a sense, decay."[2]

A SLOW DECLINE

In literary terms, *Tono-Bungay*, along with *The History of Mr. Polly*, was both an end and a beginning. It was perhaps his last novel where character and plot still predominated over the message and lessons Wells wanted to teach his readers. But after this one, Wells the novelist began to fade, while Wells the teacher, Wells the socialist, Wells the freethinker, Wells the prophet came to the forefront.

So while his writing continued, his popularity and critical reputation began a slow and steady decline. No longer content to just tell an exciting story of the future or a comic novel of the present, his mission now was to save the world. Through his books, he would show mankind how to rebuild society along socialist lines. He would preach the message of free love. He would argue the cause of the World State, a planned society that would advance the cause of science, eliminate borders between nations, and allow people to progress by their worth rather than their birth.

No cause was left unpromoted. He spoke out against organized religion. He spoke out in favor of eugenics, which meant using science to "breed" a better and stronger race of humans and using sterilization to "weed out" the weak. He spoke out against Zionism and the creation of a Jewish state. He praised Soviet dictator Joseph Stalin, saying, "I have never met a man more candid, fair, and honest."[3]

In his need to use his books to teach and to change the world, what he gave up on was his natural abilities as a storyteller. As one critic said, "Mr. Wells is a born storyteller who has sold his birthright for a pot of message."[4] Writing in his autobiography, Wells defends many of these later books such as 1919's *The Undying Fire*, a rather odd rewriting of the Book of Job, saying, "In many ways I think *The Undying Fire* one of the best pieces of work I ever did. I set great store by it still."[5]

There was still the occasional best seller. His *Outline of History*, published in 1920, was a huge success and began a new era of history books being written for a mass audience. But that book, too, became mired in controversy, when seven years after its publication a Canadian author named Florence Deeks sued Wells for plagiarism. Deeks claimed that large portions of *The Outline of History* had been taken from her own unpublished manuscript, "The Web of the World's Romance," which had sat for more than a year in the offices of Wells's North American publisher, MacMillan and Company. While the case was dismissed, some researchers today have made a serious case for Deeks's allegations, showing a large number of errors and omissions that both manuscripts shared.

PERSONAL LIFE

As Wells's literary reputation began its slow decline, so, too, did his personal reputation. A fervent advocate of free love, Wells believed that individuals should not be tied down by their marriage vows and should be allowed and even encouraged to have relationships outside of their marriage. And he lived what he preached.

Throughout his marriage to Amy Catherine, he had relationships with other women, including Margaret Sanger, an American known for her activism in promoting the use of birth control; the novelist Elizabeth von Arnim; the writer Amber Reeves, with whom he had a daughter in 1909; and most famously, the author and feminist Rebecca West, 26 years his junior, with whom he had a son, Anthony West, in 1914.

In his autobiography, Wells defends these relationships and claims that his wife was happy to allow the freedom to follow his heart. Of course, we only have Wells's word on his wife's acceptance of his relationships and children with other women. While Amy knew about many of these affairs, she remained married to Wells until her death in 1927.

He spent his later years angry at the world, frustrated that his dream of a peaceful world government had evolved into

Did you know...

The legacy of H.G. Wells as an author and a visionary is almost impossible to underestimate. One case in point is that of rocket scientist Robert H. Goddard. From childhood, Goddard was inspired by Wells's fiction to work on the science of rocketry, which was still in its infancy. His research led to the work of German scientists who developed the V2 rocket during World War II, which, in turn, led directly to the work done in the American Apollo space program that landed men on the moon in the late 1960s and 1970s.

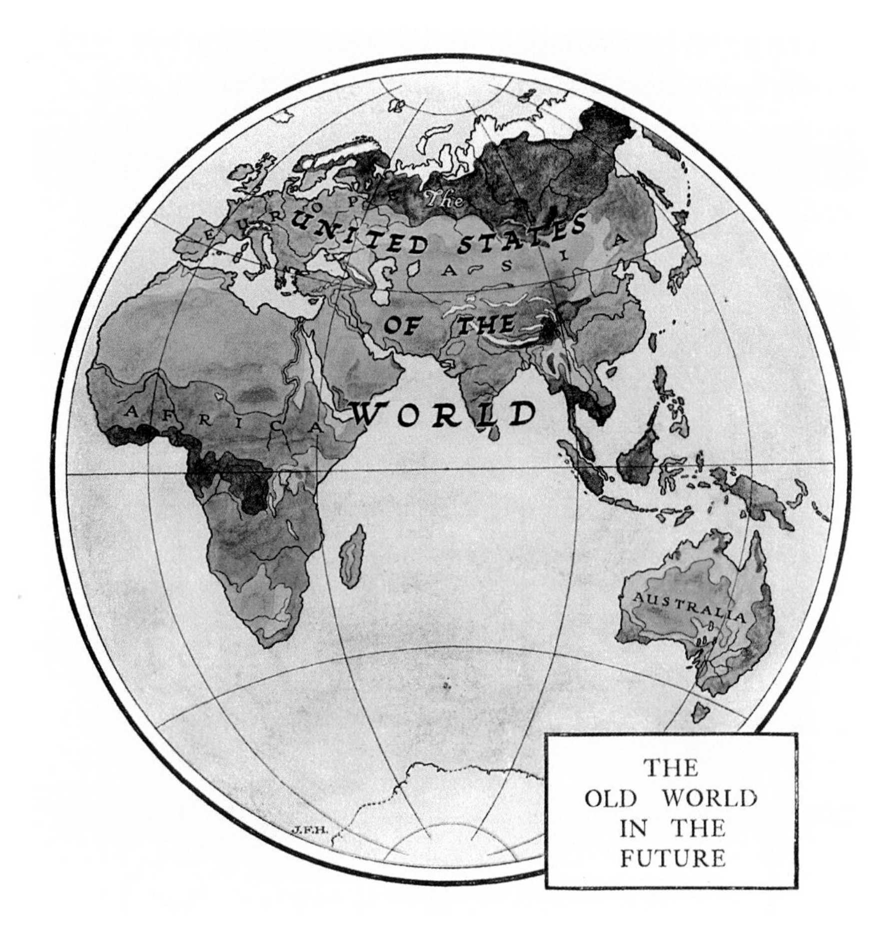

In the later years of his life, having witnessed the destructiveness of two world wars, H.G. Wells was wracked with despair that his vision of a united world* (seen here) *had not yet come to pass.

the nightmare of World War II (1939–1945), disappointed in his fading literary reputation, running unsuccessfully for Parliament, and, always, always, writing, speaking out, and never completely giving up on his dreams for a better world.

H.G. Wells died on August 13, 1946, at his home at 13 Hanover Terrace, Regent's Park, London, of unspecified causes. At the height of World War II, with bombs falling all around him during the London Blitz, the man who had long believed that mankind's baser instincts would lead to its ultimate destruction, wrote what he thought should be the words engraved on his tombstone. In the preface to the 1941 edition of his book *The War in the Air*, he wrote that his epitaph should simply say: "I told you so. You *damned* fools."[6]

LEGACY

In the words of Richard Hauer Costa, H.G. Wells "was a great writer who did not always write well. He made his reputation with—and will be longest remembered for—scientific fantasies which he never took seriously. Pushing 70, he wrote: 'It had become a bore doing imaginative books that do not touch imagination.'"[7]

But Wells was wrong. It is primarily through his scientific fantasies that he is remembered, and it is those fantasies that remain his greatest achievement. In them, the son of a failed storekeeper and his wife showed the world that, with education, with drive and determination, he could succeed. He could escape the destiny that Victorian England had laid out for him, give readers for generations to come new worlds to explore and new worlds to dream of, and fire their imaginations to create new worlds of their own.

The great Argentine author Jorge Luis Borges said it best when he wrote of H.G. Wells:

> Of the vast and diversified library he left us, nothing has pleased me more than his narration of some atrocious miracles: *The Time Machine*, *The Island of Dr. Moreau*, . . . *The First Men in the Moon*. They are the first books I read; perhaps they will be the last. I think they will be incorporated, like the fables of Theseus or Ahasuerus, into the general memory of the species and even transcend the fame of their creator or the extinction of the language in which they were written.[8]

CHRONOLOGY

1866 Herbert George Wells is born on September 21, at Bromley in Kent, England, to Joseph and Sarah Wells.

1874–1880 Wells attends Thomas Morley's Commercial Academy.

1880–1884 Fails in apprenticeships at drapers and chemists, attends school when he can, and begins teaching in preparatory school.

1884–1887 Student at the Normal School of Science, London, England. In his first year he takes classes from Thomas H. Huxley.

1888 Publishes in serial form his first major literary work, the uncompleted "Chronic Argonauts," in the *Science Schools Journal.*

1891 In October, Wells marries Isabel Mary Wells, a cousin.

1895 Publishes *The Time Machine* to widespread acclaim. Divorces Isabel Mary Wells and marries his former student Amy Catherine Robbins.

1896 Publishes *The Island of Dr. Moreau* and *The Wheels of Chance.*

1897 Publishes *The Invisible Man* and *Thirty Strange Stories.*

1898 Publishes *The War of the Worlds.*

1901 Publishes *Anticipations* and *The First Men in the Moon.* Birth of his first son, George Philip Wells.

1903 Birth of his second son, Frank Richard Wells.

1905 Publishes *A Modern Utopia* and *Kipps.* His mother, Sarah Wells, dies.

1909 Publishes *Tono-Bungay* and *Ann Veronica.*

1910 Publishes *The History of Mr. Polly.* His father, Joseph Wells, dies.

1914 First visit to Russia. Birth of a son, Anthony West, to Cicily Fairfield, today known by her pen name, Rebecca West.

1918 Promotes League of Free Nations as a means of gaining permanent worldwide peace.

1920 *The Outline of History* is published.

1922 Wells becomes member of the Labor Party. He accepts the Labor candidacy for the lord rectorship of Glasgow University but is defeated; is also defeated in his run for Parliament.

1924 Atlantic Edition of his works is published in 28 volumes.

1927 Wells's wife, Amy Catherine Wells, dies.

1934 Third visit to Russia for talk with Soviet premier Joseph Stalin. *Experiment in Autobiography* is published.

1935–1936 Writes screenplays for *Things to Come* and *The Man Who Could Work Miracles*.

1938 Orson Welles's radio broadcast of *The War of the Worlds* causes panic throughout much of the United States.

1946 Herbert George Wells dies on August 13, at the age of 79.

NOTES

Chapter 1

1 H.G. Wells, *Experiment in Autobiography*. London: Faber and Faber, 1984, p. 109.

2 Ibid., p. 76.

3 Ibid.

4 Ibid., pp. 76–77.

5 H.G. Wells, *The History of Mr. Polly*. Charleston, S.C.: BiblioBazaar, 2007, p. 170.

6 Wells, *Experiment in Autobiography*, p. 52.

Chapter 2

1 Wells, *Experiment in Autobiography*, p. 43.

2 Ibid., p. 45.

3 Ibid.

4 Ibid., p. 48.

5 Ibid.

6 Ibid., p. 49.

7 Ibid.

8 Ibid., p. 54.

9 Ibid.

10 Ibid., p. 49.

11 Ibid., p. 58.

12 Ibid., p. 60.

13 Ibid., pp. 39–42.

14 Ibid., p. 63.

15 Ibid., p. 70.

16 Ibid., p. 71.

17 Ibid., p. 74.

18 Ibid., p. 73.

Chapter 3

1 Wells, *Experiment in Autobiography*, p. 74.

2 Ibid., p. 77.

3 Ibid.

4 Ibid., p. 82.

5 Ibid., p. 84.

6 Ibid., p. 91.

7 Ibid., p. 94.

8 Ibid., p. 67.

9 Ibid.

10 Ibid., p. 108.

11 Ibid., p. 115.

12 Ibid.

13 Ibid., p. 117.

14 Ibid.

15 Ibid., p. 118.

Chapter 4

1 Wells, *Experiment in Autobiography*, p. 127.

2 Norman and Jeanne MacKenzie, *The Life of H.G. Wells: The Time Traveller*. London: The Hogarth Press, 1987, p. 35.

3 Wells, *Experiment in Autobiography*, p. 135.

4 Ibid., p. 138.

5 Ibid.

6 MacKenzie and MacKenzie, *The Life of H.G. Wells*, p. 40.
7 Ibid.
8 Wells, *Experiment in Autobiography*, p. 152.
9 MacKenzie and MacKenzie, *The Life of H.G. Wells*, p. 44.
10 Ibid., p. 47.
11 Ibid., pp. 47–48.

Chapter 5

1 Wells, *Experiment in Autobiography*, p. 199.
2 MacKenzie and MacKenzie, *The Life of H.G. Wells*, p. 53.
3 Ibid., p. 57.
4 Wells, *Experiment in Autobiography*, p. 201.
5 MacKenzie and MacKenzie, *The Life of H.G. Wells*, p. 57.
6 Ibid., p. 58.
7 Ibid., p. 57.
8 Ibid., p. 60.
9 Wells, *Experiment in Autobiography*, p. 281.
10 Ibid., p. 235.
11 Ibid.
12 Ibid.
13 Ibid.
14 Ibid., p. 236.
15 Ibid.
16 Ibid., p. 240.
17 Ibid.
18 Ibid., p. 245.
19 MacKenzie and MacKenzie, *The Life of H.G. Wells*, p. 69.
20 Wells, *Experiment in Autobiography*, p. 296.
21 Ibid.
22 Ibid., p. 297.
23 Ibid., p. 298.
24 Ibid., p. 300.
25 Ibid., pp. 304–305.
26 Ibid., p. 305.

Chapter 6

1 Wells, *Experiment in Autobiography*, p. 311.
2 Ibid., p. 314.
3 Ibid., p. 321.
4 Ibid., pp. 333–334.
5 MacKenzie and MacKenzie, *The Life of H.G. Wells*, p. 90.
6 Ibid.
7 Ibid., p. 92.
8 Wells, *Experiment in Autobiography*, p. 363.
9 Ibid., p. 371.
10 Ibid., p. 372.
11 Ibid.
12 Ibid., p. 373.
13 Ibid., p. 374.
14 MacKenzie and MacKenzie, *The Life of H.G. Wells*, p. 103.
15 Ibid., p. 105.
16 Ibid, p. 106

Chapter 7

1 MacKenzie and MacKenzie, *The Life of H.G. Wells*, p. 116.
2 Ibid.

3 Richard Hauer Costa, *H.G. Wells: Revised Edition*. Boston: Twayne Publishers, 1985, p. 10.

4 Ibid., p. 13.

5 Ibid., p. 14.

6 H.G. Wells, *The Time Machine*. Rockville, Md.: Phoenix Pick, 2008, pp. 80–81.

7 Costa, *H.G. Wells*, p. 15.

8 Ibid., p. 16.

9 MacKenzie and MacKenzie, *The Life of H.G. Wells*, p. 125.

10 Ibid., p. 126.

11 Ibid.

12 Ibid., p. 123.

13 Ibid., p. 125.

14 Costa, *H.G. Wells*, p. 19.

15 Ibid., p. 20.

16 H.G. Wells, *The War of the Worlds*, New York: Dover Publications, 1997, p. 1.

17 Costa, *H.G. Wells*, p. 23.

Chapter 8

1 MacKenzie and MacKenzie, *The Life of H.G. Wells*, p. 161.

2 Ibid.

3 Wells, *The History of Mr. Polly*, p. 170.

4 Costa, *H.G. Wells*, p. 43.

5 Ibid., p. 47.

Chapter 9

1 Costa, *H.G. Wells*, p. 57.

2 MacKenzie and MacKenzie, *The Life of H.G. Wells*, p. 244.

3 Wells, *Experiment in Autobiography*, p. 806.

4 Christopher Rolfe and Patrick Parrinder. *H.G. Wells Under Revision: Proceedings of the International H.G. Wells Symposium, London, July 1986*, Selinsgrove, Penn.: Susquehanna University Press, p. 9.

5 Wells, *Experiments in Autobiography*, p. 499.

6 H.G. Wells, "Preface to the 1941 Edition," *The War in the Air*, http://ghostwolf.dyndns.org/words/authors/W/WellsHerbertGeorge/prose/warintheair/warinairpref1941.html.

7 Costa, *H.G. Wells*, p. 148.

8 Ibid., unnumbered page.

WORKS BY H.G. WELLS

NOVELS

1895 *The Time Machine*; *The Wonderful Visit*
1896 *The Island of Dr. Moreau*; *The Wheels of Chance*
1897 *The Invisible Man*
1898 *The War of the Worlds*
1899 *When the Sleeper Wakes*
1900 *Love and Mr. Lewisham*
1901 *The First Men in the Moon*
1902 *The Sea Lady*
1904 *The Food of the Gods and How It Came to Earth*
1905 *Kipps*; *A Modern Utopia*
1906 *In the Days of the Comet*
1908 *The War in the Air*
1909 *Tono-Bungay*; *Ann Veronica*
1910 *The History of Mr. Polly*; *The Sleeper Awakes* (revised edition of *When the Sleeper Awakes*)
1911 *The New Machiavelli*
1912 *Marriage*
1913 *The Passionate Friends*
1914 *The Wife of Sir Isaac Harman*; *The World Set Free*
1915 *Bealby: A Holiday*; *The Research Magnificent*
1916 *Mr. Britling Sees It Through*
1917 *The Soul of a Bishop*
1918 *Joan and Peter: A Story of an Education*
1919 *The Undying Fire*
1922 *The Secret Places of the Heart*
1923 *Men Like Gods*
1924 *The Dream*

1925 *Christina Alberta's Father*
1926 *The World of William Clissold*
1927 *Meanwhile*
1928 *Mr. Blettsworthy on Rampole Island*
1929 *The King Who Was a King*
1930 *The Autocracy of Mr. Parham*
1932 *The Bulpington of Blup*
1933 *The Shape of Things to Come*
1936 *The Croquet Player*
1937 *Brynhhild*; *Star Begotten*; *The Camford Visitation*
1938 *Apropos of Dolores*; *The Brothers*
1939 *The Holy Terror*
1940 *Babes in the Darkling Wood*; *All Aboard for Ararat*
1941 *You Can't Be Too Careful*

SHORT STORY COLLECTIONS

1895 *The Stolen Bacillus and Other Incidents*; *Select Conversations with an Uncle (now extinct)*
1896 *The Red Room*
1897 *Thirty Strange Stories*; *The Plattner Story and Others*
1899 *Tales of Space and Time*; *A Cure for Love*
1903 *Twelve Stories and a Dream*
1911 *The Country of the Blind and Other Stories*; *The Door in the Wall and Other Stories*
1913 *The Star*
1915 *Boon, the Mind of the Race, the Wild Asses of the Devil, and the Last Trump*
1922 *Tales of the Unexpected*
1923 *Tales of Wonder*; *Tales of Life and Adventure*
1925 *The Empire of the Ants and Other Stories*
1927 *The Short Stories of H.G. Wells*; *Selected Short Stories*
1929 *The Adventures of Tommy*
1930 *The Valley of Spiders*
1931 *The Stolen Body and Other Tales of the Unexpected*; *The Famous Short Stories of H.G. Wells*

1940 *Short Stories by H.G. Wells*

1943 *The Inexperienced Ghost*; *The Land Ironclads*; *The New Accelerator*; *The Truth About Pyecraft and Other Short Stories*

SELECTED FILM STORIES

1935 *Things to Come* (adaptation of *The Shape of Things to Come*)

1936 *The Man Who Could Work Miracles*

NONFICTION

1893 *Honours Physiography*; *Text-Book of Biology/Zoology*

1897 *Certain Personal Matters*

1901 *Anticipations of the Reactions of Mechanical and Scientific Progress upon Human Life and Thought*

1903 *Mankind in the Making*

1906 *The Future in America*

1907 *The Misery of Boots*; *Will Socialism Destroy the Home?*

1908 *First and Last Things*

1911 *Floor Games*

1912 *The Great State*; *Great Thoughts from H.G. Wells*; *Thoughts From H.G. Wells*

1913 *Little Wars*; *New Worlds for Old*

1914 *The War That Will End War*; *An Englishman Looks at the World*

1915 *The War and Socialism*; *The Peace of the World*

1916 *What Is Coming?*; *The Elements of Reconstruction*

1917 *God the Invisible King*; *War and the Future* (aka *Italy, France and Britain at War*); *Introduction to Nocturne*

1918 *In the Fourth Year*

1919 *The Idea of a League of Nations* (with others); *The Way to the League of Nations* (with others)

1920 *The Outline of History*; *Russia in the Shadows*; *Frank Swinnerton* (with Arnold Bennett and Grant Overton)

1921 *The Salvaging of Civilization*

1922 *A Short History of the World*; *Washington and the Hope of Peace* (aka "Washington and the Riddle of Peace")

1923 *Socialism and the Scientific Motive*

1924 *The Story of a Great Schoolmaster: Being a Plain Account of the Life and Idea of Sanderson of Oundle*

1925 *A Year of Prophesying*; *A Short History of Mankind*

1926 *Mr. Belloc Objects to "The Outline of History"*

1927 *Wells' Social Anticipations*

1928 *The Way the World Is Going*; *The Book of Catherine Wells*; *The Open Conspiracy* (aka *What Are We to Do with Our Lives?*)

1930 *The Science of Life* (with Julian S. Huxley and G.P. Wells); *Divorce As I See It*; *Points of View*

1931 *The Work, Wealth and Happiness of Mankind*; *The New Russia*; *Selections from the Early Prose Works of H.G. Wells*

1932 *After Democracy*

1934 *Experiment in Autobiography*

1935 *The New America: The New World*

1936 *The Anatomy of Frustration*

1938 *World Brain*

1939 *The Fate of Homo Sapiens* (aka *The Fate of Man*); *The New World Order*; *Travels of a Republican Radical in Search of Hot Water*

1940 *The Common Sense of War and Peace*; *The Rights of Man*

1941 *The Pocket History of the World*

1942 *The Outlook for Homo Sapiens*; *The Conquest of Time*; *Modern Russian and English Revolutionaries* (with Lev Uspensky); *Phoenix: A Summary of the Inescapable Conditions of World Reorganization*

1943 *Crux Ansata: An Indictment of the Roman Catholic Church*

1944 *'42 to '44: A Contemporary Memoir*; *Reshaping Man's Heritage* (with J.B.S. Haldane and Julian S. Huxley)

1945 *The Happy Turning*; *Mind at the End of its Tether*; *Marxism vs. Liberalism* (with J.V. Stalin)

POPULAR BOOKS

THE HISTORY OF MR. POLLY

In this novel, considered Wells's comic masterpiece, Mr. Alfred Polly, unhappily married and dissatisfied with his life, attempts to burn down his failing shop while at the same time killing himself, which will allow his wife to rebuild and live on his insurance money. But when Mr. Polly succeeds at burning down his shop (and several others) while failing at his suicide attempt, he leaves his old life and sets out on the road in search of a new one, experiencing life for the first time before finally settling down to a new life and a new love.

THE TIME MACHINE

First published in 1895, *The Time Machine* tells the story of a man known simply as "The Time Traveller." With his invention of a "time machine," the Traveller goes forward in time to the year 802,701 and has a series of thrilling adventures with the two groups still surviving on Earth: the Eloi and the Morlocks. After escaping from the Morlocks, the Traveller goes forward in time and forward again, witnessing the planet Earth slowly go cold and die.

THE WAR OF THE WORLDS

Published in 1898, this science fiction novel looks at the invasion of Earth by Martians through the eyes of an Englishman in London. The inspiration for many science-fiction films, it has itself been turned into a movie, most recently in 2005's *War of the Worlds* directed by Steven Spielberg and starring Tom Cruise. Perhaps its most famous incarnation, though, was the 1938 radio broadcast by Orson Welles, which led many to believe that Martians had actually invaded the United States, causing panic throughout much of the country.

POPULAR CHARACTERS

ALFRED POLLY

The hero of Wells's 1910 comic masterpiece, *The History of Mr. Polly*, Mr. Polly, a fictional character derived in part from both Wells and his father, Joseph, sets out to escape a life in which he feels trapped for one in which he can feel free and happy.

EDWARD "TEDDY" PONDEVERO

The uncle of George Pondevero, the hero of Wells's 1909 novel, *Tono-Bungay*, Uncle Edward, the inventor of the fraudulent cure-all Tono-Bungay, is presented by Wells as being all-too human, always on the lookout for ways to make money, always seeking new ways to promote Tono-Bungay and new conditions that he falsely claims it will cure, among them seasickness and influenza.

GRIFFIN

The "Invisible Man" from Wells's 1897 novel of the same name, Griffin (his first name is never mentioned) is a brilliant scientist who develops a treatment that makes his body invisible. Unable to reverse the process, Griffin slowly goes mad and sets out to use his invisibility to rule the world, before finally being killed by local villagers.

BIBLIOGRAPHY

Costa, Richard Hauer. *H.G. Wells, Revised Edition*. Boston: Twayne Publishers, 1985.

MacKenzie, Norman, and Jeanne MacKenzie. *The Life of H.G. Wells: The Time Traveller*. London: The Hogarth Press, 1987.

Wells, H.G. *Experiment in Autobiography*, Vols. 1 and 2. London: Faber and Faber, 1984.

———. *Works of H.G. Wells*, New York: Random House Value Publishing, 1988.

FURTHER READING

Books

Gosling, John. *Waging the War of the Worlds: A History of the 1938 Radio Broadcast and Resulting Panic.* Jefferson, N.C.: McFarland, 2009.

Holmsten, Brian, and Alex Lubertozzi. *The Complete War of the Worlds.* Naperville, Ill.: Sourcebooks MediaFusion, 2001.

McConnell, Frank. *The Science Fiction of H.G. Wells.* New York: Oxford University Press, 1981.

Nesbitt, E. *7 Books in 1: The Railway Children, Five Children and It, The Phoenix and the Carpet, The Story of the Amulet, The Story of the Treasure-Seekers, The Would-Be-Goods, and The Enchanted Castle.* London: Shoes and Ships and Sealing Wax Ltd., 2004.

Web Sites

The H.G. Wells Society
http://www.hgwellsusa.50megs.com/

The Literature Network: H.G. Wells
http://www.online-literature.com/wellshg

PICTURE CREDITS

page:

10: Hulton Collection/Getty Images
18: © Mary Evans Picture Library/The Image Works
26: © Mary Evans Picture Library/The Image Works
30: The Granger Collection
36: The Granger Collection
40: © Mary Evans Picture Library/The Image Works
45: Bridgeman Art Library
50: Alamy
57: The Granger Collection
63: © Mary Evans Picture Library/The Image Works
66: Bridgeman Art Library
71: Fotosearch/Getty Images
78: © Fortean/Topham/The Image Works
88: © Ann Ronan Picture Library/HIP/The Image Works
92: Hulton Archive/Getty Images
98: © NMPFT/Daily Herald Archive/SSPL/The Image Works
102: © NMPFT/Daily Herald Archive/SSPL/The Image Works
108: © Mary Evans Picture Library/The Image Works

INDEX

ABOUT THE CONTRIBUTOR

DENNIS ABRAMS is the author of numerous books for Chelsea House, including biographies of Barbara Park, Che Guevara, Rachael Ray, Xerxes, Georgia O'Keeffe, Nicolas Sarkozy, Hillary Rodham Clinton, Jay-Z, Albert Pujols, and L. Frank Baum. He attended Antioch College, where he majored in English and communications. He lives in Houston, Texas, with his partner of 21 years, three cats, and a dog named Junie B.